Goldwin Smith

Irish History and Irish Character

Goldwin Smith

Irish History and Irish Character

ISBN/EAN: 9783744717366

Printed in Europe, USA, Canada, Australia, Japan

Cover: Foto ©ninafisch / pixelio.de

More available books at **www.hansebooks.com**

IRISH HISTORY

AND

IRISH CHARACTER.

BY

GOLDWIN SMITH.

Oxford & London:
J. H. AND JAS. PARKER.
1861.

Printed by Messrs. Parker, Cornmarket, Oxford.

PREFACE.

THIS sketch is an expansion of a lecture delivered before the Oxford Architectural and Historical Society at their Annual Meeting in June 1861. It would serve a good purpose if it should fall into the hands of any popular writer on Irish history, and induce him to pay more attention than writers on that subject have generally paid to general causes, to cultivate the charities of history, and, in the case of the rulers as well as of the people, to take fair account of misfortunes as well as of crimes.

IRISH HISTORY AND IRISH CHARACTER.

THE history of Ireland from the Conquest to the Union is the miserable history of a half-subdued dependency. Its annals are the weary annals of aggression on the one side, and of rebellion on the other; of aggression sometimes more, sometimes less cruel and systematic, of rebellion sometimes more, sometimes less violent and extensive, but of aggression and of rebellion without end. Few are the points, few are the characters of moral interest in such a story. It is a long agony, of which the only interest lies in the prospect of its long-deferred close. Yet a knowledge of these events must be of the highest practical importance to those who may be called upon to deal, as rulers or landlords, with the Irish people.

The destiny of the country has, to some extent, been written on its face by nature. It is a large island, close to a much larger island, which lies between it and the main-land. The course of its history could not fail to be greatly influenced by the history of its more powerful neighbour. It was almost certain, in the primitive age of conquest, to be subdued. Yet, from its magnitude, it was almost certain not to be subdued without a long and painful struggle. Had it been a third part of the size, its independence would have expired without a pang. Moreover, the channel between the two islands, though steam has now bridged it over, was broad enough to form, in the infancy of navigation, a considerable impediment to the arms of an English conqueror; more especially as the nearest point of contact with England was Wales, a mountainous district, remote from the early seats of English wealth and power, and one which itself long remained unsubdued.

Britain itself is cut in two by the Cheviots and the wilds of the Border; whence its inhabitants were naturally divided into two nations with separate histories. Ireland is in closer contact with the northern division; and in the earliest times it exerted great influence on Scotland, if it was not, as seems most probable, the mother-country of the Gael. In later times Scotland has exerted great influence on Ireland. Ulster has, in fact, become a part, not so much of Keltic and Catholic Ireland, as of Saxon and Presbyterian Scotland.

England being interposed between Ireland and France, the continental country to which Ireland lies most open is Spain. By Spain, in the sixteenth century, the most determined efforts were made to detach Ireland from England. The architecture of the old houses in the town of Galway, and the gay and graceful dresses of the neighbouring peasantry, are by some supposed to recal the time when that town was the port of a Spanish trade; a trade which was so prized as a source of wealth, that for an act of piracy committed on a Spanish vessel, a mayor of Galway, with Roman spirit, hanged his own son over his own gate. The mansions of little merchant princes which once emulated the luxury and the jealousy of Seville, have sunk into Irish squalor and decay: but from the coast of

Galway the fisherman still sees a visionary shore rise out of the Atlantic; a dreamy recollection, perhaps, of Spain, realized again in the New World.

The siren pamphleteers of France may sing as they will of the fitness of Ireland for all kinds of agricultural produce; of her self-sufficing variety of wealth, and of the immense population which she might maintain if she would only listen to disinterested advice, and facilitate the influx of the requisite capital by rebellion and civil war. According to all trustworthy economists, those of France included, Ireland is a grazing country. "The whole island," says M. de Lavergne[a], speaking of Ireland in former times, "then formed but one immense pasture, which is evidently its natural destination, and the best mode of turning it to account." The same writer remarks that the herbaceous vegetation of Ireland is admirable, and that it is not without reason that the trefoil has become the heraldic emblem of the *green isle*. The vast Atlantic clouds, which soften the hues and outlines of the scenery, drop fertility on the grazing lands, and clothe the mountains high up with the brightest verdure. On the other hand, it is difficult, over a great part of the island, to get in a wheat harvest. The true agricultural wealth of the country is displayed in the great cattle-fair of Balinasloe. Its natural way to commercial prosperity seems to be to supply with the produce of its grazing and dairy farms the population of England; a population which is sure, from the quantity of coals and minerals beneath the surface of

[a] *Essai sur L'Économie Rurale de l'Angleterre de l'Écosse et de l'Irlande,* p. 385.

the country, to be very large in proportion to the agricultural area. The notion that a country can supply all its own wants, like the Stoic notion that each man can be complete in himself and self-sufficing, is a mischievous dream. For the purposes of the great human community, nations and men alike have been so made as to be dependent on each other.

The growth of flax and the linen manufacture form a variety in the occupations of the people, and, as a natural consequence, modify their intellectual character; and when the influx of capital shall enable the Irish thoroughly to work the various coal-fields, another new social element of an important kind may perhaps be introduced. The mining element generally appears destined to remain of subordinate importance.

As a commercial country Ireland is furnished with excellent harbours, and with a superabundance of internal water communication. But she pays a heavy price for her lakes and rivers in having nearly a seventh of her area covered with bog. The broad and brimming Shannon, half lake, half river, is fed by the vast and wasteful bog of Allen.

The dampness of the climate, while it is the source of vegetable wealth and of vegetable beauty, could not fail to relax the energies of the people, and to throw them back in the race of nations for pre-eminence in things requiring physical exertion. We see this when we compare the early history of the Irish with that of the Scandinavians, braced to daring and enterprize by the climate of the North. These influences weigh heavily on man in the infancy of civilization: in its more advanced stages they are in a great degree subdued and neutralized by the sovereign power of mind.

In estimating the wealth of a country, we must not leave out of sight its beauty. Beauty is a kind of wealth which grows more valuable as civilization advances. As the life of man becomes busier, and more beset by care and turmoil, he longs the more for the refreshment afforded by the silent and pensive loveliness of nature, which his increasing refinement of mind and sensibility render him at the same time more able to appreciate. Ireland with its beautiful coasts, and its hideous central flats and bogs, has been compared to an ugly picture set in a rich frame: but the frame is rich, both in loveliness and in wildness. Killarney has already been almost rifled of the charm of solitude by the crowd which escapes from our great cities; and as the wealth of Ireland increases and the passage between the two islands becomes shorter and easier, the villas of nobles and merchant princes which now rise in the Highlands of Scotland, may rise in Connemara, which, if it does not equal the Highlands in romantic beauty, has charms of its own in the exquisite balminess and purity of its air and in the poetry of its immense and lonely sea.

Of the physical influences which affect the character and destiny of nations, the most important seems to be that of race. We need not here inquire whether peculiarities of race spring from an actual diversity of origin, or whether they were superinduced upon the common type of humanity by the different circumstances under which different primeval families or tribes were placed.

That which it is important always to remark in touching on this subject is, that peculiarities of race, however strong, are not indelible. There is a considerable difference, as we shall have occasion to notice, between the character of the mass of Irishmen and that of the mass of Englishmen; but between individual Irishmen and Englishmen who have received the same education, and lived in the same society, the difference is not perceptible: and the same influences which produce a complete assimilation in certain cases may, if extended to the whole of both races, produce it in all. Nor do the differences of natural character between different races bear any proportion to the common elements of human nature in all. Nations may become depraved in heart or understanding; but when they are not depraved the reason and the conscience of all nations are the same, and the same Christian religion suits them all, in London, in Paris, and in Otaheite.

Professed ethnologists must determine whether there are any ethnological facts at all corresponding to the stories which fill the opening chapters of every history of Ireland about the successive immigrations of Firbolgs, Tuatha-na-Danains, and Milesians. There are certainly considerable differences of form and complexion among the Irish people. The dark and somewhat small, though graceful peasantry of Connemara, present a strong contrast to the tall gaunt form and rather light complexion which mark the typical Irishman of Tipperary. But there has been a large infusion of foreign blood even in the south; and differences of food, climate, and other physical influences may have done the rest.

To the eye of the historian the popular history of primitive Ireland is all the more fabulous because it is extremely circumstantial, and even affects accuracy of dates and numbers. When there is any genuine tradition, fancy is controlled by it : when there is none, she revels freely in the void. Genuine tradition, preserved by memory and oral repetition, is of necessity meagre and vague. When the exact date of a king or dynasty anterior to Abraham is confidently given us, we may be sure we are in the region of the creative imagination. Nor is there any process known to criticism by which these vast piles of tinted cloud can be condensed into a modicum of solid fact; for one part of the story rests on no better evidence than the other parts. To assume that of so many statements some must be true, is to assume that there cannot be such a thing as a vast tissue of fable. The name *traditions* begs the question, when the interval between the alleged event and the first record of it is more than ten times that which we find to be the ordinary limit of human memory, and when there is no other evidence of accurate transmission.

"It is more than probable," says the judicious Mac-Geoghegan, "that Ireland remained desert and uninhabited from the Creation to the Deluge." But the Irish chroniclers confidently tell us of an immigration previous to the Flood.

Nevertheless, these fictions, rivalling in extravagance those of Egypt and China, possess interest as characteristic creations of the national fancy; they stand in marked contrast to the brief and matter-of-fact records of the Anglo-Saxon Chronicle, to the graceful legends which sprang from the awakening intellect of Greece, and to those, so instinct with policy, legislation, and the discipline of war, so like the real history of a conquering nation, which form the Roman mythology of Rome.

The sure test of language proves that the native Irish were a portion of the great Keltic race which once covered all Britain as well as all Gaul, and probably Spain. This race, swept from the plains of England and the lowlands of Scotland by the conquering Teuton, found a refuge in the Welsh mountains, in the hill country of Devonshire and Cornwall, and in the Highlands of Scotland; but its great asylum was Ireland. In Ireland we probably see its peculiarities in their most native and genuine form. In France, where it has reached its highest pitch of greatness, and most fully developed its tendencies and capacities, its natural character has been greatly modified by external influences, especially by the influence of Rome, both as an empire and as an imperial Church.

In the primeval struggle of races for the leadership of humanity, the Keltic race for the most part ultimately succumbed; but it was a mighty race, and at one moment its sword, cast into the scale of fate, nearly outweighed the destiny of Rome. The genius of Cæsar at last decided in favour of his countrymen a contest which they had waged at intervals during four centuries not merely for empire, but for existence. Not only did the Kelts vanquish in the battle-fields of Italy, at Allia, at Thrasymene, and at Cannæ, and bring Rome to the extremity from which she was saved by Marius; they carried their terrible arms into Greece, sacked Delphi, and founded as conquerors their principalities in Asia Minor. They met the summons of Alexander with gasconading defiance; they overthrew the phalanx in the plains of Macedon. The most brilliant and reckless of mercenaries, they filled the armies of the ancient powers, and Carthage had her Keltic soldiery as modern France had her Irish brigade.

M. Martin, the French historian of France, says, speaking of the Kelts of that country[b],—" From the beginning of historic time, the soil of France appears peopled by a race lively, witty, imaginative, eloquent, prone at once to faith and to scepticism, to the highest aspirations of the soul and to the attractions of sense; enthusiastic and yet satirical, unreflecting and yet logical, full of sympathy yet restive under discipline, endowed with practical good sense, yet inclined to illusions; more disposed to striking acts of self-devotion than to patient and sustained effort; fickle as regards particular things and persons, persevering as regards tendencies and the essential rules of life; equally adapted for action and for the acquisition of knowledge; loving action and knowledge each for its own sake; loving above all war, less for the sake of conquest than for that of glory and adventure, for the attraction of danger and the unknown; uniting, finally, to an extreme sociability, an indomitable personality, a spirit of independence which absolutely repels the yoke of the external world and the face of destiny." A critic might say that in this portrait of the Kelts by a Kelt is unconsciously depicted a point of character which is

[b] Vol. xvi. p. 658.

not named. Vanity is a quality which the French hardly disclaim, and which indeed, by partly creating the superiority which it implies, has helped to enable them to do great things. It might also be asked, whether by "practical good sense" is meant only a certain clearness of view, dexterity and tact, or the highest practical wisdom; for of the highest practical wisdom the political history of France can scarcely be called an example. Those violent oscillations, again, between unreasoning faith and a scepticism almost as unreasoning, and between extremes of all kinds, to which M. Martin points, may lend an exciting interest to French history, and amuse, while they trouble the world; but the race which is conscious of such tendencies will do well, if it aspires to real greatness, not to boast of them, but to correct them.

Different fortunes and different institutions have, however, as was before said, produced a great difference of character between the French and the Irish Kelt. The French Kelt is all lightness and gaiety of heart; but in the Irish Kelt there is, besides the hilarity, the conviviality, the love of fun, a strain of melancholy, which belongs to the same lively and emotional temperament, and which finds a charming expression in the "Irish Melodies" of Moore. The effect of despotism, whether political or ecclesiastical, is, by interdicting to the people grave subjects of thought, to produce a childlike carelessness of disposition, which shews itself in the perpetual pursuit of gaiety and pleasure. In the case of the French Kelt both political and ecclesiastical despotism have been at work, and they have produced their natural effect. In the case of the Irish Kelt the circumstances of his country and his Church have conspired to preserve the sadder part of the character only too well; and in him, close beside the source of laughter, still flows the fountain of tears.

From the loss of the melancholy and pensive element of the common nature, the poetry of the French is, in the main, a mere poetry of art. France has had masterpieces of taste and correctness in her Corneilles and Racines, but she has scarcely produced a poet so touching as Moore.

The Keltic race readily took to the rhetorical part of Roman education; and rhetoric is a peculiar gift both of the French and the Irish mind, nor is it wanting to the descendants of the Welsh Cymry or the Scotch Gael. It is unhappily a bane as well as a gift; and much that is called eloquence in Ireland, perhaps not a little that is called eloquence in all countries, is mere extravagance and violence of language, the mark not of genius, but of want of sense and self-control. The excesses of French rhetoric do not in substance fall short of the excesses of Irish rhetoric; but from assiduous literary culture they have assumed a polished and classical form, and the French rhetorician avoids those strained metaphors and violations of metaphor by which the best efforts of Irish orators have been disfigured. No speaker trained in the school of French taste would commit such offences against the rules of taste as were committed by Curran, by Grattan, and even by Burke. Those who blame Burke's party for not putting him in a high place of responsibility should consider the extravagant violence and absurdity of some of his rhetorical sallies. Nor, again, would any French speaker but a Jacobin indulge in the rabid invective which disgraced the debates of the Irish Parliament and formed a main part of the oratory of O'Connell.

The source of Irish *bulls* is a national quickness of wit which, when uncontrolled by judgment and education, tumbles, in its haste, into laughable blunders. Such a bull as "The minister had a majority in everything but numbers" is merely a lively idea expressed without reflection.

Cruelty and recklessness of human life seem the qualities of a fiend. But it will be found that, like indulgence in violent invective and other uncontrolled exhibitions of passion, they are often connected less with deep depravity than with a most wretched kind of weakness. They may often be classed among those infirmities to which the Latin language gave the expressive name of *impotentia*. The civil wars, the religious persecutions, the revolutions of French history are marked by these qualities in their worst form; and the same may be said of the civil wars, rebellions, and agrarian insurrections of Ireland. The delirium of bloodthirstiness extended to the Irish women in O'Neil's massacre, and in the Wexford massacres of 1798. In the same manner French ladies are recorded to have looked on with horrible pleasure at executions in the civil war of the Burgundians and Armagnacs, and in that of the League; and women were among the most constant and exulting spectators of the guillotine. The allusion in Shakspeare's "Henry IV." to the Welsh women who frantically mutilated the bodies of the slain after the defeat of Mortimer's army, is historical; and this atrocity may be classed among the instances of a sort of demoniac possession to which weak natures are exposed.

M. Martin, in the passage above quoted, admits that the French Kelts are more distinguished by a power of making extraordinary efforts than by perseverance, the palm of which he tacitly surrenders to their Teutonic rivals. There seems no good reason for believing that the Irish Kelts are averse from labour, provided they be placed, as people of all races require to be placed for at least two or three generations, in circumstances favourable to industry. They are capable of great endurance and of great abstinence. It is true that when they seek enjoyment it is rather in the shape of excitement than of comfort. What an Englishman wants to make him happy, it has been said, is a full belly and a warm back; what an Irishman wants to make him happy is a glass of whiskey and a stick. But it is difficult to distinguish the faults of the Irish from their misfortunes. It has been well said of their past industrial character and history, — "We were reckless, ignorant, improvident, drunken, and idle. We were idle, for we had nothing to do; we were reckless, for we had no hope; we were ignorant, for learning was denied us; we were improvident, for we had no future; we were drunken, for we sought to forget our misery. That time has passed away for ever." No part of this defence, probably, is more true than that which connects the drunkenness of the Irish peasantry with their misery. Drunkenness is, generally speaking, the vice of despair; and it springs from the despair of the English peasant as rankly as from that of his Irish fellow. The sums of money which have been lately transmitted by Irish emigrants to their friends in Ireland seem a conclusive answer to much loose denunciation of the national character, both in a moral and in an industrial point of view.

As Ireland is, in its agricultural produce, the supplement of England, so are the endowments of the Kelt the supplement to those of the Saxon. What the Saxon wants in liveliness, grace, and warmth, the Kelt can supply; what the Kelt lacks in firmness, judgment, perseverance, and the more solid elements of character, the Saxon can afford. The two races blended together may well be expected to produce a great and gifted nation; and it would probably detract from our greatness and from the richness of our national gifts if the Keltic element of the united people should be too much drained away by unlimited emigration. It was not without a providential object that the earth was so laid out with island, mountain, and morass, as to give refuge to remnants of the weaker races in the primeval era of wandering and conflict, when the open country was swept by the conquering inroads of the strong. The warm friendships so often formed between characters the most diverse prove that in diversity of character there is a fundamental sympathy beneath a superficial antipathy. Between the Kelt and the Anglo-Norman or Anglo-Saxon, the diversity of character was great. The antipathy therefore was strong, and long and cruel has been the process by which it has been in part worked off. But we shall come to the source of sympathy at last.

The primitive form of Irish society was the sept or clan, the next grade in the ascending scale of political progress to the patriarchal state, the lineaments of which it to a great extent preserves; the chief being in fact the father of the clan, whose members all, like members of a family, bear the same name. This form of society seems to have been common to the whole Keltic race. It subsisted nearly down to our own time among the Keltic Gael of the Scotch Highlands, and determined, by its peculiar nature, the action of the Highland population in our last great civil contests. It prevailed in Wales previous to the final subjugation of that country and the complete introduction of Anglo-Norman laws and institutions. The population of ancient Gaul and Britain was, in like manner, divided into a number of clans or septs, varying in numbers and power, with which the Romans contended, and from which, acting singly or in loose and fickle coalitions, they encountered the same fitful and unsteady, yet protracted resistance which Scottish kings encountered from the Gael, the Plantagenets from the Cymry, and the Anglo-Norman colonists of Ireland from the chiefs of the native septs.

The clan, however, seems to have varied considerably in the distinctness of its form under different local circumstances and at different periods of its existence. In the glens of Scotland, fenced in by mountains, each clan would naturally be kept separate, compact, and independent. The same would be the case among the hills of Wales. But in a plain country intermixture and fusion would occur; the original tie of blood would give place to one merely of name; and the sentiment of the clansman would consequently grow weaker. At the same time, the chiefs of the more powerful clans would obtain a permanent ascendancy, and the transition from a cluster of independent clans to a monarchy would begin. Such seems to have been the course which matters were taking in Gaul when it was invaded by the Romans, and in Ireland when it was invaded by the Danes and Normans. The possession of horses, and the consequent rise of a sort of military aristocracy of horsemen or charioteers, must also have tended to break up in Gaul, Britain, and Ireland the equality of the clansmen and the brotherhood of the clan. In the Highlands the chief clansmen necessarily continued to fight on foot by the side of the humblest members of their clan.

The process of fusion and consolidation had advanced so far in Ireland that the country was divided into five principalities; while above these principalities a supreme monarchy had begun to struggle into existence, though it had not yet finally settled in any one house. The great bogs or forests in the centre of the island must have presented a serious obstacle to complete union. On the other hand, union was promoted, for a time at least, by the incursions of the Danes, which made the natives feel the necessity of having a single commander. The greatest of the kings of all Ireland was styled Brian of the Tribute; and tribute, rather than regular jurisdiction, seems to have been the prerogative of the kings. In like manner the chiefs of the more powerful clans in the Highlands exacted tribute from the less powerful without bringing them regularly under their jurisdiction. The memory of the united monarchy and of the assemblies of its chiefs, priests, lawgivers, and bards lingers round the great mound of Tara, where a fond imagination has placed the princely halls of ancient Irish state, where the national cause of Ireland has more than once rallied, and where O'Connell put on his mock crown. The memory of the Principalities dwells in that most striking monument of antiquity, the rock crowned with its cathedral, its palace, and its round towers, which rises from the plain of Cashel.

In the Septs we probably see the origin of the ridiculous factions among the Irish peasantry, the Caravats and Shanavests, the Two-Year Olds, and Three-Year Olds, which have scarcely yet ceased to "trail their coats" to each other. It is not long since the police was called upon to stop a fight between the Two-Year Olds and the Three-Year Olds. The original source of the feud between those factions is supposed to have been a dispute about the age of a young bull; but the spirit of division and combat dates from the primitive institutions of the race. The divisions of counties seem to have partly succeeded, as ties of faction, to the divisions of septs.

The abode which Greek fancy feigned for the gods, and the life of enjoyment which it assigned to them, were but the counterpart of the abode and the life of a Grecian prince. The fairy-land of the Irish has its factions and its faction fights. There are the Donegal fairies, the Kerry fairies, the Limerick fairies, and the Tipperary fairies; and an Irishman once helped the Kerry fairies to gain a great victory over the Limerick fairies and was rewarded for his assistance by a fairy cap[c].

There appears to be in the Keltic race a strong tendency to what is called Imperialism, as opposed to the Constitutionalism to which the Teutonic races tend. The Teuton loves laws and parliaments, the Kelt loves a king. Even the highly civilized Kelt of France, familiar as he is with theories of political liberty, seems almost incapable of sustaining free institutions. After a moment of constitutional government he reverts, with a bias which the fatalist might call irresistible, to despotism in some form, whether it be that of a Bonaparte or that of a Robespierre. The Irish have hitherto shewn a similar attachment to the rule of persons rather than to that of institutions. So far as willingness to submit to governors is concerned, they are only too easily governed. Loyalty is the great virtue of their political character. Its great defect is want of independence and of that strong sense of right by which law and personal liberty are upheld. These are the characteristic qualities of clansmen, to whom, in their half-patriarchal state, the will and the protecting power of the chief are more than any law. But whether it was the clan that engendered the political tendency of the Keltic race, or an innate tendency of the race that

[c] Kohl's Ireland, p. 34.

produced the clan, or at least preserved that form of society when it had been discarded by other races, is a question which cannot here be considered. It opens a wider and a most interesting question, of a general kind, as to the historical relation between the characters of different races and their different primitive institutions.

The direct and manifest influence of the clan feeling, and of the feeling towards the chief of the clan, reaches far down into Irish history; and it is probable that its indirect and secret influence is not yet extinct.

We see the different political tendencies of the Irish and English races combined, yet distinguishable from each other, in the political character of Burke, to whose writing we owe, more than we are aware, the almost religious reverence with which we regard the Constitution. Trained among English statesmen, Burke had learnt to love English institutions, but he loved them not like an Englishman, from a practical sense of their usefulness, but like an Irishman, with the passionate fervour of personal attachment, and rendered to their imagined founders, collectively, the homage of the heart which devoted loyalty pays to a king. His feelings, diffused by his eloquence, have become those of our whole nation.

The Sept land belonged not to the individual septmen, nor to the chief, but to the sept. It may be taken as a fact pretty well proved in historical philosophy that common ownership of land preceded separate ownership, in many cases if not in all [d]. The village communities of Russia and of Hindostan still hold their land in

[d] See Maine, On Ancient Law, p. 260.

common. A trace of the original state of things is seen in the agrarian laws of Rome and in those redistributions of the land among all the members of the State which occur in Greek history, and which seemed to Greek statesmen revolutionary but not immoral. Traces of the cognate institution of the Clan are seen in the Roman clientage and in the divisions of Greek communities into tribes with rites commemorative of a supposed tie of blood. The transition from common to separate ownership is no doubt closely connected with the transition from the pastoral to the agricultural state: the flocks and herds of a tribe graze together, but the plot which a man has tilled and sowed with his own hands becomes his own. This transition is a great step in human progress; and one which every nation, to become civilized, must take. But it cannot be assumed that the separate ownership of land, and all its attendant legal relations and obligations, are articles of natural morality, innate in every human breast; or that an imperfect reverence for them must be everywhere a mark of depravity, and everywhere provoke the just vengeance of the law. They are, on the contrary, improvements gradually introduced as society emerges from the primitive state. They are natural to man in the sense of being good for him; but they are not natural to man in the sense of being among the most simple and rudimentary ideas of the human mind. They require to be commended to his respect and affection by long experience of their beneficial effects. Have their beneficial effects been long experienced by the Irish peasantry? Has property in land, according to the

English system, presented itself to him in the course of
his history as in the form of security, independence,
domestic happiness, dignity and hope? Has it not
rather presented itself to him in the form of insecurity,
degradation, and despair? It would be too much to say
that modern Irish agrarianism is the direct offspring of
primitive Irish institutions; but it is not too much to
say that even modern Irish agrarianism is rather the
offspring of a barbarism prolonged by unhappy circumstances and bad government than of anything more
deserving of unqualified indignation.

The chiefs, indeed, had demesne lands attached to
their chieftainries; but both the chieftainry and the
demesne went not by regular descent, nor by will, but by
a qualified election, which was confined to the members
of the chief family, but among the members of that
family was free; so that an uncle or a brother would be
preferred to an infant or feeble son. To the Anglo-
Norman lawyers the custom of Tanistry, as it was called,
could only appear mere barbarism. "In England,"
says Sir John Davis[e], "and all well-ordered common-
wealths, men have certain estates in their lands and
possessions, and their inheritances descend from father
to son, which doth give them encouragement to build
and to plant, and to improve their lands, and to make
them better for their posterities. But by the Irish custom of Tanistry, the chieftains of every country, and
the chief of every Sept, had no longer estate than for
life in their chiefries, the inheritance whereof did rest

[e] A Discovery of the True Causes why Ireland was never Subdued
and brought under Obedience of the Crown of England.

in no man. And these chiefries, though they had some portions of land allotted unto them, did consist chiefly in cuttings and cosheries, and other Irish exactions, whereby they did spoil and impoverish the people at their pleasure. And when their chieftains were dead, their sons or next heirs did not succeed them, but their Tanists, who were elective and purchased their elections by strong hand; and by the Irish custom of Gavelkind the inferior tenancies were partable amongst all the males of the Sept, both bastards and legitimate: and after partition made, if any one of the Sept had died, his portion was not divided among his sons, but the chief of the Sept made a new partition of all the lands belonging to that Sept, and gave every one his part according to his antiquity."

The English courts of law in the reign of James I. adjudged tanistry to be "no estate, but only a transitory and scambling possession;" an adjudication in which Sir John Davis, moderate and sensible as he is, entirely acquiesces. He is also clearly of opinion that the Sovereign is not only authorized but bound to take the strongest measures, if necessary, to "reduce his people" from such "barbarism" to "civility." Our jurists in India have found the same difficulty in recognising as anything but "a scambling possession" the Hindoo custom of succession by adoption.

It is not easy to find in writers on the subject an explicit statement as to the occasions on which, and the limits within which, the chief exercised the patriarchal power, to which Sir John Davis alludes, of making a new partition of the Sept land. "It seems impossible," says Mr. Hallam, "to conceive that these partitions were renewed on every death of one of the sept; but," he adds, "they are asserted at least to have taken place so frequently as to produce a continual change of possession." To whatever extent the power may have been exercised, it was no doubt the relic of a state of things when all the possessions of the patriarchal community were held in common under the authority of the patriarch, and was analogous, as was before intimated, to the agrarian laws of Greece and Rome.

Mr. Hallam suggests, as one of the sources of this policy of repartition, a too jealous solicitude as to the excessive inequality of wealth. This seems too artificial a motive to have actuated septs just raised above the nomad state. But there appears to be something in the Keltic character, as developed in the French people, which loves the social equality arising from minute subdivision of property, as well as the equal submission of all the members of the State to the despotic government of a common chief.

The passage above quoted from Davis, and his general account of the Irish, having been written in the reign of James I., shew how completely the series of calamities and disturbances had arrested the social and economical development of the Irish people at an almost primitive stage.

Progress had been made, however, previous to the Conquest, towards that system of separate property in land which marks advanced civilization. Not only had the Septs apparently quite emerged from the nomad state and become confined each to its own settlement, which is the first step of all; but as between the members of the Sept there seems to have obtained a right of occupancy, subject to the power of redistribution vested in the chief, but otherwise amounting very nearly to property, like the occupancy of the public land at Rome. The land which a member of the sept had occupied seems generally to have passed at his death, as a matter of course, to all his sons. The Welsh chiefs received from their retainers certain dues or stated gifts, which were rather minutely regulated by law [f]. The Irish chiefs seem to have received dues or gifts of the same kind, though they indulged themselves largely in coshering, or free quartering, on their retainers. But there is a wide step between this state of things and the English relations of landlord and tenant, with a certain rent paid annually and regular eviction in case of non-payment. Under the sept system there would be abundance of tyranny, violence, arbitrary exaction, and perhaps of vindictive expulsion by offended chiefs, but not the legal process of eviction. "It is a common use," says Spenser [g], "amongst landlords of the Irish to have a common spending upon their tenants ... for they were never wont and yet are loath to yield any certain rent, but only such spendings; for their common saying is, 'Spend me and defend me.'" If "Spend me and defend me" is not still the common saying of the Irish peasantry towards their

[f] See Walther, *Das Alte Wales*.

[g] State of Ireland. From the context of the passage Spenser seems not to understand so clearly as Sir John Davis the phenomena before him; for he identifies the relation between chief and clansman with the English "tenancy at will."

landlords, it is probably still, to a great extent, their common feeling. It is difficult at least to say at what period of their social history they can have been thoroughly trained to understand and respect relations between landlord and tenant of a more regular and commercial kind. They may still, as in the time of Spenser, be "loath to yield a certain rent;" but at the same time it appears that they are as ready as ever to be "spent" by a chief who will "defend" them; and they seem not unwilling to accept a resident landlord as a chief. The state of society described in the Irish tales of Miss Edgeworth is essentially a clannish state. The dependents feel that they owe personal devotion to their superior as the price of personal protection; and to pay that devotion in unstinted measure is the highest social morality which they know. When an absentee landlord applies to them the screw of the Middleman, and expects them to recognise the embodiment of social morality in its pressure, he appeals to a sentiment belonging to a more mature and regular state of society, and one which the people cannot, without a longer and more kindly education in these matters, be reasonably expected to possess.

The Anglo-Norman lawyers looking for an explanation of everything in their own system of tenures, and seeing that in Ireland there was no primogeniture, naturally identified the Irish practice with the peculiar Kentish custom of gavelkind. But there was nothing in Kentish gavelkind analogous to the Irish repartition; nor did bastards, as in Ireland, take their share.

Attachment to a chief is an almost necessary step in

political progress between attachment to the father of a family and attachment to the State; and in like manner sept ownership is an almost necessary step between mere nomad occupation and the civilized freehold. In a political as well as in an economical point of view the Irish people may be considered as having been arrested at a certain stage of development, and prevented by a series of calamities from advancing in the ordinary course.

The traces of Irish Druidism seem rather obscure. Yet it can scarcely be doubted that the religion of the Irish was the same as that of the other Kelts. The holy fire which was kept burning down to the suppression of monasteries in a small cell near the church of Kildare, and attended by virgins, is held to have been a relic of the holy fires of the Druids[h]. It at once reminds us of the vestal fire at Rome. At all events, it seems certain that religious enthusiasm and a corresponding reverence for the ministers of religion were qualities deeply seated in the primitive character of the Irish race. The same qualities under a different form are seen in the Gaelic Cameronians and in the Welsh Methodists, who are almost as much under the dominion of their preachers as the Irish peasant is under the dominion of his priest; and who almost rival Irish Catholicism in the wildness of their superstitions. In France the people, originally religious and devoted to religious objects and enterprises, have, owing chiefly to the corruption of the Church in the last century, undergone one of those violent reactions to which the enthu-

[h] See Logan's Gael, ii. 326.

siastic temperament is liable; and their devotion has been turned from the Church to the nation, and its aggrandizement and glory.

Historical accidents have made the Irish enthusiastic adherents of the Papacy; but the essence of their religious character, as we see from the analogy of their Keltic brethren, is enthusiasm alone. Mr. Francis Newman in his "Phases of Faith" has described from his personal observation the effect produced on the Irish peasantry by the enthusiasm and asceticism of a Protestant clergyman, who was able, within the range of his ministry, to draw away the hearts of the people from their priests. On the other hand, it seems probable that no religion which is cold and formal, whatever be the articles of its creed, will easily make proselytes among a Keltic race.

The Keltic nature is communicative even to excess. England has kept her revolutions to herself; France proclaimed hers universal, and endeavoured to propagate it over the world. The French may claim the credit of having been the great transmitters of ideas between the different nations of Europe. When Christianity, preached by St. Patrick, touched the heart of the Irish Kelts, it kindled in them such a flame of enthusiasm, that they sent out apostles into all lands. Not only the holy islands of Iona and Lindisfarne, the cradles, in a wild time of war and rapine, of Christianity in Northern Britain, but the name of St. Gall in Switzerland is a monument of a great missionary Church, the glory of which filled France, and which brought the tidings of salvation to the Lombards of

Italy and to the heathens of the Maine and the Upper Rhine. 'Fridolin the Traveller,' and the others who 'travelled' on the same errand, were perhaps partly impelled by a national love of wandering; but this love of wandering was a necessary instrument which Christianity in early days adopted, and made its own for the conversion of mankind. As the Irish Church sent forth the Gospel into other countries, so it received with eager hospitality into its own all who desired to be instructed in the Word of Life, or in such other knowledge as those who were called learned in that day possessed. The Keltic intellect, when under education, outstrips the Teutonic as the laurel outstrips the oak ; and Saxons came for instruction to the schools of Armagh, and to that melancholy plain where the Shannon flows by the lonely ruins of Clonmacnoise. Charlemagne appreciated in the Irish preachers and scholars powerful instruments of the civilization which it was his mission to promote. He gave some of them places of honour in his court, and employed them in the instruction of Frankish youth. Scotus Erigena was sitting, a familiar guest, at the table of Charles the Bald, when the King asked him how far a *Scot* was removed from a *Sot*, and he answered, with Irish wit, "By a table's breadth." During the seventh and eighth centuries and part of the ninth, Ireland played a really great part in European history. It was the bright morning of a dark day.

The Keltic intellect is subtle, inquisitive, and fond of the metaphysics of religion. The Gael of the Highlands loves the mystical reasonings of Calvinism as well as its awful denunciations; and the same religious taste is evinced by the Methodists of Wales. This is not a habit of mind which tends to the observance of orthodoxy. Ireland produced the first great heretical teacher of the Middle Ages, in the person of John Scotus Erigena, the father of all who take the Protestant view of the Eucharist. Feargall, or Virgilius, an Irishman who was appointed by Pepin Bishop of Salzburg, enjoys, somewhat doubtfully, the credit of having earned the honour of astronomical heresy by maintaining, to the scandal of the orthodox Boniface, and of the Holy See which he represented, that the earth was round, and that there were other men under our feet.

The division, however, which undoubtedly existed between the Keltic Church in Ireland, Wales, and Scotland, on the one hand, and the Churches which were under the complete dominion of Rome, on the other, was not so much a division of doctrine as of ecclesiastical jurisdiction and discipline. But in those days the outward unity of Christendom, which was still struggling for existence against masses of heathenism, was a matter of vital importance; and differences of ecclesiastical jurisdiction and discipline,— questions as to the time of keeping Easter, as to the exact mode of administering Baptism, as to uniformity in dress and tonsure among the soldiers of that which was truly a militant Church, —may well have appeared, even to the strongest and most spiritual minds, far graver than charity can allow them to be in our time. The Irish Church was a thing external to Catholic, as Irish society was to feudal, Europe. It was an irregularity, an anomaly, an eye-sore to all ecclesiastics who lived under and loved the imperial unity and the perfect order of the Church of Rome. In the person of Colman it had contended against Rome, represented by Wilfrid, for the spiritual allegiance of the Anglo-Saxon Church of Northumberland. At the decisive Synod of Whitby, in the dispute touching the rule of keeping Easter, Colman pleaded the authority of Ireland's great Saint, Columba. "Will he," replied Wilfrid, "set the authority of Columba in opposition to that of St. Peter, to whom were given the keys of heaven?" "Do you acknowledge," said King Oswio — whose adherence was the prize of the debate—to Colman, "that St. Peter has the keys of heaven?" "Unquestionably," replied Colman. "Then, for my part," said Oswio, "I will hold to St. Peter, lest, when I offer myself at the gates of heaven, he should shut them against me." It is vain to deny that there was a difference between the Church of St. Peter and Wilfrid, for which Oswio pronounced, and that of St. Columba and Colman, which he rejected. Without venturing into the controversy about the Culdees, it may be pretty safely said that Irish monachism, though abounding in fervour, was not disciplined after the Roman rule; and that the introduction of the regular Cistercians, by St. Malachy, under the auspices of St. Bernard of Clairvaux, seemed to a strict Churchman a great ecclesiastical reform. St. Bernard was the moral dictator of the Catholic Church in the early part of the twelfth century, and none could represent with more authority the sentiments of the Catholic world as to the character of any person or institution. He speaks of St. Malachy, the Romanizing reformer of the Irish Church, as of one who had cleared and cultivated an ecclesiastical wilderness [1] :—"The man of God, on entering into his bishopric, found that it was not to men, but to beasts, that he was sent. The like he had never seen even in the lowest barbarism: never had he met with any so rude in manners, so disorderly in the performance of worship, so impious in creed, so barbarous in their laws, so stiff-necked under discipline, so foul in life. They were Christians in name, Pagans in deed. They paid no tithes nor first-fruits ; they did not enter into lawful wedlock, nor practise confession ; there was none found anywhere to ask penance or to impose it. There were very few ministers of the altar; yet what would have been the use of more, since the laity gave those few almost nothing to do ? They could hope for no fruit from the performance of their duties among that wicked people. For neither the voice of the preacher nor of the singer was heard in the churches." Afterwards, through the reforming efforts of the Saint, "Rudeness gave way, barbarism was allayed; and that rugged race began gradually to be softened, gradually to admit correction and submit to discipline. The barbarous rule was put away; the Roman rule was introduced; the customs of the Church were everywhere received; the contrary customs were rejected; the cathedrals were rebuilt; the clergy were ordained in them ; the sacramental rites were duly performed ; con-

[1] De Vita S. Malachiæ, c. 8.

fessions were made; the people came together to the churches; and the shame of concubinage was done away by the general use of marriage;—in fine, all things were so much changed for the better, that it might be said of that nation, in the words of the prophet, 'A people which before was not Mine is become My people.'" St. Anselm, in his expostulatory letter to an Irish prince [k], uses language which is less strong but not less decided. Giraldus Cambrensis denounces the Irish, in regard to matters of religion, as a "most vile nation,—a nation that wallowed in every vice, a nation that of all nations was most uncultivated in the rudiments of the faith:" but his specific charges are that they do not pay tithes or first-fruits; that they neglect the rite of marriage; do not come to church; and marry the wives of their deceased brothers [l]. These are partly offences against Christianity, but they are partly offences against Rome.

The Church is not a disembodied spirit, but a spirit embodied in human society; and its state in any particular society cannot fail to be affected by the state of civilization. As to the civilization of the Irish, Giraldus says, with epigrammatic bitterness, that they lived on beasts, and were as the beasts they lived on, ("Gens ex bestiis solum et bestialiter vivens.") This severe sentence contains its own explanation. If the Irish were still in the pastoral state, as the words of Giraldus imply, they could scarcely fail to be brutish. Bread is the staff of civilization as well as of life. In a people of herdsmen and hunters, living each with his

[k] Anselm, Ep. 147. [l] Top. Hibern., cap. 19.

war-hatchet—the precursor of the modern shillelagh—in his hand, and filling the country with their clan feuds and raids, the Church must have been like "a lodge in a garden of cucumbers." Its position must have been aptly represented by those Round Towers, the subjects of so much romance and mystery, which are now allowed to have been half bell-towers, half refuges for the priests and the sacred things when the district was swept by plundering incursions.

The hierarchy of the primitive Irish Church was most imperfect to a Roman eye. For a long time there were no Archbishops. Bishops were multiplied with what to Roman eyes was most irregular prodigality[m]. There seems to have been one in every village. But they were consecrated, against the Roman rule, by one bishop only. Hence their ordinations were questionable; and the Roman Churches looked askance on clergymen from Ireland with uncertain credentials, as a strict Anglican Bishop might at the present day.

The absence of towns, which was fatal to the political and social progress of the country, no doubt also greatly affected the regular organization of the hierarchy, the settlement of sees, and the pomp and order of religious worship. The only towns of any consequence in Ireland before the Conquest were those on the East and South coast occupied by the Danes.

The feudal system, in the countries where it prevailed, laid hold on the episcopate, and turned the bishoprics into baronies and the rich sees into appanages for great feudal houses. In the same way the Sept seems

[m] S. Bernard, De Vita S. Malachiæ, c. 10.

to have laid hold on the episcopate in Ireland. St. Bernard[a] complains of "a most pernicious custom, which had gained strength by the diabolical ambition of men in power, of holding bishoprics by hereditary succession. For they would suffer none to be bishop who was not of their own tribe and house." "This execrable succession," he says, "had gone great lengths. The evil had continued for fifteen generations. And to such an extent had a wicked and adulterous generation confirmed to itself this depraved right, or rather this wrong, deserving the punishment of the worst death, that though clergymen of their blood sometimes failed, yet bishops of it never failed. In fact, eight married men, unordained, though lettered, had preceded Celsus (in the see of Armagh)." Cormac, King of Munster, whose chapel stands on the rock of Cashel, was at once Bishop and King, patriarchally uniting the spiritual with the temporal chieftainship of his tribe. If this was irregular and unseemly, it had its counterpart, at least, in the Elector-Bishops of the great German sees.

The chiefs also, as we learn from the reforming Canons of the Synod of Cashel, denied to the clergy those immunities from lay taxation and jurisdiction which the clergy, wherever they had arrived at a sense of their corporate position, claimed as essentially belonging to the spiritual caste; and which, under the dictatorship of the Pope, they were for a time able, to a great extent, to secure throughout Romanized Christendom.

It is from the earth itself that the salt of the earth

[a] De Vit. S. Malach., c. 10.

is taken. The Irish Church could draw its clergy only from wild clansmen, full of violent lusts and passions, and of all the weakness of barbaric natures. Giraldus praises the Irish clergy in many things, especially for their chastity and for their remarkable power of fasting. But we can believe him without difficulty when he says that after fasting nobly all day they were apt to get drunk at night.

A curious charge made by the Romanizing party against the native Irish Church was, that though it had among its saints many confessors, it had no martyr. When this was cast in the teeth of an Irish prelate at the time of the Conquest, the martyrdom of Becket being then recent, he readily answered that the reproach of his Church would soon be removed, for a race had now come among them who were good hands at making martyrs.

The wildness of the native character also infected the Church with wild superstitions, which have left their trace even down to the present time. The Purgatory of St. Patrick, the entrance to the other world, placed in an island on Loch Derg, reminds us of the cave of Trophonius, and evinces a most primitive simplicity and coarseness of the religious imagination.

The form of St. Patrick himself is almost lost in a halo of extravagant and miraculous legends. The fact is, that deep religious feeling and an extraordinary degree of religious self-devotion are found in the hearts of barbarous converts; but the intellectual element of religion, which consists in the love of truth, can scarcely come into existence till a nation has undergone an intellectual training such as the Irish could not be said in the primitive ages of their Church, and can scarcely be said now, to have received.

Neither was it scandalous or unparalleled if the remains of actual heathenism lingered beside the rites of Christianity; if in the rites with which covenants were ratified the authority of saints' relics was mingled with the pledge of blood; if certain prayers and invocations retained a taint of the worship of the sword and fire; if the right arm was left unchristened that it might be more terrible in war; if funerals were celebrated with orgiastic wailings for the dead; if, as William of Newbury says, the septs collected by plundering raids the means of keeping a glorious Easter. Giraldus notes that even the Irish saints appeared, like the Irish themselves, to be remarkably vindictive. They were made after the image of a half-Christianized people.

Cæsar, if his account is true, found in Britain certain septs who had exaggerated the sept connexion into one of family by a barbarous community of wives and children. The Irish custom of "fosterage" may perhaps have been intended to bind the members of the sept together by a sort of family connexion of a more innocent kind. This strange bond was so strong that we hear of a chieftain dying of grief for the loss of his two foster-brothers. At the execution of a traitor at Limerick, Spenser saw an old woman, the traitor's foster-mother, "take up his head whilst he was being quartered, and suck up the blood that ran from it, saying that the earth was not worthy to drink it, and steep her face and breast with it, at the same time tearing her hair, and crying out and shrieking most terribly." This heathen fancy mingled itself with Christianity. The connexion of sponsorship or gossiprede was made a sort of second fosterage; and fosterage and gossiprede with the Irish are alike denounced by English statutes. Cambrensis says bitterly, that "as for their own brothers and kinsmen, the Irish persecute them when living unto death, and avenge them when slain; while such love and fidelity as they shew is confined to their foster-brethren and foster-children." The strength of the artificial tie would inevitably detract from that of natural affection. It was observed by those versed in Irish government, that to take a chief's children or kinsmen as hostages was of little use [o]. Yet the natural force of family affection in the Irish, according to those who have observed them most closely, is not small, but remarkably great.

It must be allowed, however, that the testimony of St. Bernard, St. Anselm, and Giraldus Cambrensis is concurrent and strong as to the incontinence of the primitive Irish, and their disregard of the marriage tie. And this evidence is confirmed by that of Sir John Davis, who speaks of "their common repudiation of their wives; their promiscuous generation of children; their neglect of lawful matrimony,"—vices which he couples with "their uncleanness in apparel, diet, and lodging, and their contempt and scorn of all things necessary for the civil life of man." This looseness in regard to matrimony may be viewed in connexion with the disregard of legitimacy in elections to chieftainships

---

[o] See *Desiderata Hibernica Curiosa*, vol. ii. p. 111.

and apportionments of land: probably each of the two habits prolonged and aggravated the other.

The habitual perfidy which Giraldus charges the Irish with having shewn, in spite of the horrid rites with which their covenants were sealed, may be partly accounted for by the charity of history in a similar manner. The bond of the sept was still too powerful and exclusive to admit an enlarged sense of public faith, which does not arise till the moral horizon has been expanded so as to take in the State and, at last, the great community of mankind.

Spenser, complaining of the untrustworthiness of the Irish peasantry as jurymen, says that "they care much less than the others [the English] what they swear, and sure their lords may compel them to say anything; for I myself have heard, when one of the baser sort (which they call churls) being challenged and reproved for his false oath, hath answered confidently, That his lord commanded him, and it was the least thing that he could do for his lord to swear for him." "So unconscionable," he adds, "are these common people, and so little feeling have they of God or their own soul's good." Spenser's own barbarous ancestors would have done the same thing. There is a wide difference between this savage but disinterested devotion of body and soul to a chief, when the chief is the highest known object of earthly reverence, and interested perjury committed by the citizen of a civilized state. The former is in fact the wildness of the stock out of which, when brought under culture, the virtue of the citizen will grow.

M. Amédée Thierry, in his "History of the Gauls [p],"
says that the life of a Gallic noble in the first and
second centuries was a continual whirl of faction and
intrigue. The same might have been said in a ruder
sense of the life of an Irish chief before the Conquest.
Nor would the transition to ordered civil life have been
accomplished in this case, any more than in the case of
other countries, without a painful struggle. But Irish
nationality died in its infancy, and a fond imagination,
in painting the life which would have been in store for
it, fulfils every promise of good, and leaves out of
sight everything that portended evil.

One of the great virtues of a chief in such a state of
society is a lavish hospitality, which the community
does not yet perceive to be kept up at its own expense.
The petty court of the Irish chieftains was the resort
not only of their own clansmen, but of privileged
strollers and parasites of various kinds, including the
order of strolling bards. The sociability of the Keltic
nature shewed itself in the familiarity with which the
chief seated himself at the board among his retainers.
It was with difficulty that, when transferred to a feudal
court, he could be induced to conform to the aristocratic
exclusiveness of feudal state. The Irish squire of the
last century had scarcely degenerated in these respects
from the old Irish chief.

More sinister guests in the chief's quarters than
strollers and parasites were the mercenary soldiers, or
Gallowglass, whom the chieftain seems to have kept in
his pay for the same purposes for which each clansman

[p] Vol. i. p. 461.

kept his axe. The existence of these mercenary bands must have both injured the character of the sept itself as a union of patriarchal affection between chief and clansman, and have tended greatly to delay the formation of a regular monarchy and the ascendancy of law.

In speaking of the loose rule of inheritance in the succession to land, we have noticed the equally loose custom of Tanistry in succession to the chieftainship of the Sept. Not only was the successor elected without regard to any regular order of preference between the members of the principal family, or to legitimacy; but he was commonly elected during the lifetime of the chief. Such a practice, which placed an expectant and a rival beside each petty throne, could not fail to be the source of constant disturbance among fiery and jealous natures.

The state of society which was practically so lawless was not however without the idea or the forms of law. There were Brehons, or professional judges, distinct from the chiefs, though probably not independent of them; a separation of the judicial from the political power which forms an important step in the civil development of a people. The Brehon law, of which these judges were the oracles, appears to have been a precise and elaborate code, displaying something of that peculiar aptitude for the forms of legislation which the French Kelt has displayed in the Code Napoleon, and which may exist as an intellectual gift apart from the strong moral qualities which maintain personal right, liberty, and justice. The English Statutes denounce the Brehon law as "no law, but a lewd custom;" and so, in truth, it was, when adopted, in place of the common law, by the degenerate English of the Pale: in itself it was a national code.

It is needless to say that the Eric, or pecuniary composition for blood, in place of capital or other punishment, which the Brehon law sanctioned, is the reproach of all primitive codes and of none. It is the first step from the license of savage revenge to the ordered justice of a regular law.

The legendary accounts of early Irish civilization glitter with gold and silver; and the time before the Conquest is looked back on as one of Utopian splendour and prosperity. The darkness of the present has lent brightness by contrast to the vista of the past. It is not in the evening waters of Lough Neagh alone that the oppressed and unhappy peasant

"Sees the Round Towers of other days
In the wave below him shining."

The power of hope is not extinguished in man: it turns to memory when it has no object of its own.

Among the Irish Kelts as well as among the Kelts of Gaul the products of fancy and ingenuity appear to have outrun the more substantial accessories of wealth and civilization. The only towns deserving of the name, as was before mentioned, appear to have been those of the Danes. Corn was grown; but, partly from the nature of the climate, in small quantities. The fondness for drinks sweetened with honey gave bee-keeping an important place among the articles of Brehon law, as well as among the germs of peaceful life and civilization. Commerce had raised her head, and the productions of a pastoral country were bartered for the wines of Spain and France: but the Irish do not seem themselves to have ventured on the sea, though they had coracles for the lake and river; and probably the chief traders were the Danes. The gold which museums of Irish ornaments display in such surprising quantities, appears, according to the best opinions, to have been gathered from the streams of Wicklow. Whether coined money was of early introduction seems to be still a moot point. Building with hewn stone and cement was confined to ecclesiastical edifices. Perhaps the very facility with which stone was obtained, while it has caused the island to be strewn with the wrecks of hasty habitations of different ages, may, by rendering it unnecessary to hew stone from the quarry, have checked the growth of regular architecture. The savage requires to be driven to his first tasks by nature.

On the other hand, the ancient Irish ornaments display singular taste and skill. The same qualities are displayed in the well-known forms of the Irish crosses. They emerge again after an eclipse of centuries in the beautiful carvings with which the native genius of Irish artists has adorned the Museum of Trinity College Dublin and the Museum at Oxford. Nor can it easily be doubted that an aspiration after the beautiful conspired with the object of security to produce the taper and graceful forms of the Round Towers. The play of religious fancy shews itself in the groups of Seven Churches which so frequently mark holy spots. But this cunning of hand and this fancy need to be wedded to some higher gifts of creative power in order to raise them to the level of Greek and Italian art.

The legendary authors of Greek civilization, Orpheus, Mercury, Amphion, all had for their talisman the harp. Giraldus shews that he is not a bigoted libeller of the Irish by the praises which he bestows upon their incomparable skill in music [q]. The bards, the ancient brethren of the Druids, had preserved the sanctity of their order into Christian times. They were trained by a long course of study and probation for the sacred order. The highest reverence attended them, and their malison was almost as terrible as the curse of a priest; so that the race of a man whom a bard had laid under his ban were supposed to emit from their bodies the evil odour of the accursed. These are the germs of intellectual life, germs which are small, but pregnant with mighty consequences. This is the faint beginning of that literary empire which culminated in the apotheosis of Voltaire. The bards in Ireland, as in Wales, being the guardians of national feeling and tradition, were priests of the national cause, and, as such, were banned by the Statutes of the conquering race. When, towards the close of the last century, the spirit of Irish independence woke again, though in a somewhat factitious form, two or three of the old wandering race of harpers were found, and brought to a patriotic music-meeting at Belfast. These, the last survivors of their race, delivered the harp of Ireland to Thomas Moore, in whose hands it became a powerful awakener of political sympathy for an injured

[q] Top. Hib., c. 11.

and unhappy nation, and assisted in no slight degree the cause of justice and emancipation.

We come to the Conquest, the point at which the patriot historians of Ireland raise a death-wail over the fortunes of their country. Assuredly it was the beginning of a long train of almost unexampled calamities, not to Ireland alone, but to both nations. If retribution is not, as some have maintained, the great law of history, history bears unfailing witness to the certainty of retribution.

There are certain philosophers, of a somewhat coldly scientific school, who look upon man as a creature to be organized; and who, if a conquest tends to bring a schismatical civilization within that more than Papal uniformity which they desire to impose on the world, are inclined to regard it with unmixed complacency. There is another school, of which M. Augustin Thierry is the great exponent, which draws no distinction between the international morality of the twelfth century and the nineteenth, but condemns the enterprises of Norman conquerors as vehemently as it would condemn a rapacious attack made by one civilized nation on another at the present day. This school, moreover, takes the cause of all conquered nationalities under its generous protection; and loves independence so much, and uniformity so little, that it would not only restore the Heptarchy, if it could, but the Ancient Britons.

Thus much must be admitted: there was an era when, if conquest was not moral, it was in the eyes of all men far less immoral than it is now, and when it served the object, which we can scarcely regard as otherwise than providential, of infusing new life into the effete Roman world, and moulding the great nations which have become the organs of modern civilization; when, moreover, it acted as the rude school of certain robust qualities which lie at the foundation of human character, though they require to have reared upon them a superstructure of gentler virtues. The conquest of which we are here speaking lies, in point of time, upon the very verge of this era, and is therefore among those the morality and the good effects of which are most open to question. It was, moreover, a conquest not of Christians by worshippers of Odin, or of Mahometans by Christians, but of Christians by Christians. Yet it was directly sanctioned by him whom all the Christian world then regarded, and whom the bulk of the Irish people still regard, as the Vicar of Christ, and the oracle of morality to Christendom. Not only so, but it partook in his eyes and in those of all the faithful of the character of a crusade.

It was simply the sequel of the Norman conquest of England. In the Norman conquest of England, Hildebrand, the soul of the Papacy, had been the partner of William. The Pope had sent a ring and a consecrated banner to the faithful champion of Rome, who went forth, not only to win a kingdom for himself and his followers, but to reduce the irregular and half-schismatic Church of the Anglo-Saxons to the perfect obedience and order of the Holy See. The anathemas of the Papacy against the accursed race who did not pay Peter's pence, who incestuously confounded secular with spiritual jurisdiction, and whose archbishops assumed the pall without the authority of Rome, went before the host of the Normans to victory at Hastings. In the same manner, Adrian, by that Bull which is the stumbling-block and the despair of Catholic historians, granted Ireland to the king of orthodox England, who, "as a Catholic king, was intent on enlarging the borders of the Church, teaching the truth of the Christian faith to an ignorant and rude people, and extirpating the roots of vice from the field of the Lord; and who for the better execution of this purpose, required the counsel and favour of the Apostolic See." "We, therefore," said the Pontiff, "looking on your pious and laudable design with the grace which it deserves, and favourably assenting to your petition, do hold it good and acceptable that, for extending the borders of the Church, restraining the progress of vice, for the correction of manners, the planting of virtue, and the increase of religion, you enter this island, and execute therein whatever shall pertain to the honour of God and the welfare of the land; and that the people of this land receive you honourably and reverence you. as their lord: the rights of their churches still remaining sacred and inviolate; and saving to St. Peter the annual pension of one penny from every house." Are Catholics filled with perplexity at the sight of Infallibility sanctioning rapine? They can scarcely be less perplexed by the title which Infallibility puts forward to the dominion of Ireland, the subject of its gracious grant. The Pope proclaims himself lord of Ireland because it is an island, and "all islands on which Christ the sun of righteousness hath shone undoubtedly belong to the See of St. Peter." But this perplexity arises entirely from the assumption, which may be an article of faith but is not an article of history, that the infallible morality of the Pope has never changed. The infallibility of the Pope, morally speaking, must be said by history to consist in this, that though he changes, he does not repent.

It is not the Saxon that is responsible for the conquest of Ireland, but the Norman. At that time the Saxon himself lay crushed under the Norman yoke. The conquerors were those fierce Scandinavian rovers whose incomparable energy and daring had carried them from Greenland and Iceland to the shores of the Mediterranean; who after centuries of wandering piracy had founded principalities in Normandy and Italy, and putting on the name and faith of Roman Christianity without putting off the adventurous restlessness of the pirate, had become the most devoted and valiant soldiers of the great Roman theocracy, and the leaders of its crusades against schismatics and infidels in Palestine, in England, and in Ireland, from the banks of the Jordan to the banks of the Boyne. We do not take its criminality from injustice, nor its sting from suffering, when we shew that any particular event is part of a more general movement of history; but we transfer the question to a calmer region of discussion, and disarm special resentment, at least in reasonable minds. Ireland was struck by the last languid wave of a deluge of conquest which had overwhelmed all the neighbouring nations.

Nor was this the first time that she had been trodden by a Scandinavian conqueror. The Northmen had visited her, as well as England, before the Norman invasion, when their Pagan swarms issued fresh from their native seats. If the ravages of the Danes in Ireland were less desolating than in England, it was because there was less to desolate. For a moment their terrors overcame the spirit of rivalry among the Irish chiefs, and united the forces of the assailed nation under Brian Boroihme, the Alfred of Ireland, and the hero and martyr of that vast and shadowy conflict between the two races which raged from the dawn to the evening of Good-Friday on the battle-field of Clontarf. Even in that patriotic struggle, jealousy and treachery were not absent on the Irish side. The Danes, though defeated, were not expelled; their towns on the seacoast remained almost the only towns in Ireland. They perhaps partly compensated for the evils of their alien presence by being the chief agents of trade; but they certainly, in Ireland as in England, broke the power of resistance, and opened the door for the complete success of the Norman invader.

It appears that at the time of the Conquest Ireland was full of English slaves. The Irish ecclesiastics assembled at Armagh concluded that this offence it was which, moving the wrath of Heaven, had called down upon the land the just judgment of the Conquest. These slaves had been brought by pirates, and by merchants who were probably not very clearly to be distinguished from pirates in that day. It is certain that slavery existed among the clans[r]; and this, if we do not agree

[r] See a regulation for the dress of slaves, (among other classes,) made by an ancient Irish king, in "The Four Masters," by O'Donovan, vol. i. p. 45.

with the judgment of the Council of Armagh, tends to rob them of the sympathy which might attach to defenders of personal liberty.

As to the sanctity of national independence, it is doubtful at least whether such an idea had at that time assumed a distinct form in the mind of any nation. Personal oppression and cruelty of course touched every heart, but it would perhaps be difficult to produce from any chronicler of the medieval period an expression of anguish such as would now be felt at the loss of national dignity and honour.

The Saxon Chronicle says that had William the Conqueror lived two years longer, he would have won Ireland, and that without stroke of sword. One of the two confederate powers which took part in the Conquest had been actively at work before the time of Henry II. The great propagators of the Roman doctrine and discipline, Lanfranc, Anselm, St. Bernard as the adviser of St. Malachy, the Popes themselves, had been weaving their meshes round the Irish Church. Irish kings had listened to the fatherly flattery of Roman Churchmen. A bishop of Dublin had sought consecration at the hands of an Archbishop of Canterbury; a Papal legate had been admitted in the person of Gillebert, bishop of Limerick, who had put forth a charge expounding to the Irish dissidents the canonical customs, "to the end that those diverse and schismatical orders wherewith in a manner all Ireland was deluded might give place to one Catholic and Roman office[a]." The ecclesiastics most open to these diplo-

[a] Usher, Syll. Ep. xxx.

matic attempts were those of the Danish towns, both from their isolated position and from their Norman blood and sympathies. But so far as Irish Churchmen may have been accomplices in the invasion of their country they stand by no means without excuse. They might well think that in placing Ireland under a king who was a faithful son of Rome, they were conferring on its people a benefit at least as great as that which they were to receive in the shape of emoluments and immunities for themselves. It was scarcely possible that the highest minds of that age should imagine any mode of promoting civilization so effectual as the establishment of ecclesiastical order; or that any ecclesiastical order should appear perfect but that of the Church of Rome.

Henry procured the Bull for the Conquest of Ireland as soon as he had mastered the anarchy which he found prevailing in England on his accession to the throne: but his attention being diverted by other enterprises he kept it by him for future execution. Meantime the mine was accidentally fired by a spark from another quarter. When Britain was a Roman province, an Irish chief driven from his country in a feud had come to Agricola burning for revenge, and persuasively urged that a small force would suffice to subdue Ireland. With the same vindictiveness, Dermot, when his lust and tyranny had driven him from his chieftainship, sought the aid of some Norman adventurers settled in Wales who had lightly squandered the wealth which they had lightly won, and were ready as lightly again to set forth in quest of new dangers and fresh plunder. It was an untoward circumstance at the outset that the foundation of the Norman dominion in Ireland was laid by private adventurers, instead of being laid in a more comprehensive spirit under the auspices of an able king. Mere self-interest, rapacious and irresponsible, was the guise in which the English connexion first appeared on Irish soil.

The resistance offered by the native chiefs was feeble compared with that which was offered by the Saxons to the Norman conquerors of England. The most stubborn stand was made by the inhabitants of the Danish towns. There was no protracted and wavering battle like that of Hastings. The loose Irish armies more than once flung their naked bodies, their feeble targets, and their clumsy swords on the mailed and disciplined Norman ranks; but the issue of the struggle was scarcely more doubtful than that of the struggle between the Spaniards and the Mexicans. Superiority in war, produced by better weapons and tactics, and by a greater aptitude both for obedience and of command, is in early times a high test of comparative civilization: and thus, in early times, conquest in some degree justifies itself as the ascendancy of a civilizing power.

Giraldus has given us a minute account of the personal appearance and the character of Strongbow. The countenance of the renowned adventurer was feminine, and his voice was thin; "he was gentle and courteous in his manners; what he could not gain by force he gained by address; in peace he was more ready to obey than to command; when not in battle was more a soldier than a general, in battle more a general than a soldier; always took his companions into counsel and undertook no enterprise without their advice; in action was the sure rallying-point of his troops; and of unshaken constancy in either fortune of war, neither to be disturbed by adversity nor to be thrown off his balance by success." Strongbow's Irish ally, Dermot, is described by the same writer "as tall and huge; warlike and daring, with a voice hoarse from shouting in battle; desiring to be feared rather than loved; an oppressor of the noble, a raiser up of the low; tyrannical to his own people and detested by strangers; one who had his hand against every man and every man's hand against him." His followers, after a victory, having thrown a heap of heads at his feet, the savage clapped his hands with delight, yelled forth his thanks to God, and seizing by the hair and ears a head which he recognised as that of a hated enemy, he tore off part of the nose and lips with his teeth. Without insisting on the details of the two portraits, we have no difficulty in recognising the first as typical of a conquering race, the second as typical of a race destined to be conquered.

Henry soon became jealous of the progress of his subject's arms in a realm which he had marked out for his own. Moreover, after the murder of Thomas à Becket, he probably felt that some great achievement in the cause of Holy Church was necessary in order to restore his reputation in the eyes of scandalized Christendom. He accordingly passed in person into Ireland, and produced by his majestic presence the effect which the presence of greatness has never failed to produce on Irish minds. As he moved over the country in his state and power, the chiefs bowed their heads in submission before the "son of the Empress," the greatest of all the sovereigns of his time, and not among the least of those in history. He kept his Christmas at Dublin with politic splendour. A palace had been built for him of wood and wicker-work, the counterpart on a larger scale of the palaces of Irish chiefs; and in its skilful and graceful texture he might admire the cunning of hand with which his new subjects were endowed. Had he remained to complete the conquest and organize it with the same statesmanship which had restored order to England after the anarchy of Stephen, one of the darkest leaves might have been torn from the book of fate. But scarcely had he received the lip homage of the chiefs who thronged his Christmas court, and the half submission, sent through a proxy, of the king of Connaught, then supreme king of Ireland, when the tidings of domestic rebellion called him to end elsewhere his chequered and storm-tossed, but on the whole illustrious, life. Ulster, which had not yet even nominally submitted, he was fain to grant to John de Courci, on condition that he should conquer it. "He departed out of Ireland," says Sir John Davis, "without striking one blow or building one castle, or planting one garrison among the Irish: neither left he behind him one true subject more than those he found there at his coming over, which were only the English adventurers spoken of before, who had gained the port towns in Leinster and Munster, and possessed some scopes of land thereunto adjoining, partly by Strongbow's alliance with the Lord of Leinster, and partly by plain invasion and conquest." That "inconstant sea-nymph," whom, to borrow the conceit of the same writer, "the pope had wedded to him with a ring," was as lightly lost by the departure of her new lord, as by his coming she was lightly won.

In the upshot, Henry placed the title of Lord of Ireland in his royal style before the Duchies of Normandy and Aquitaine: under him, and as his nominal tributary, the king of Connaught remained king of Ireland, in the same manner in which the princes of Wales retained their principality under the kings of England, lords of Wales: that part of the island which was occupied by the adventurers, consisting of a small district round Dublin and some ports along the south and east coasts, was taken under the direct dominion of the king of England, placed under the feudal law, and organized on the feudal system; the rest remained in the jurisdiction of the native chiefs, and under the Brehon, or Irish law. The pope was still, according to the Papal theory as to the dominion over islands, and by the admission implied in Henry's acceptance of the Papal grant, suzerain of the whole; and he was invoked by subsequent kings of England to protect them with the arms of the Church in the enjoyment of his gift.

Henry did not neglect the religious part of his enterprise, or shew himself ungrateful for the sanction it had received from the Head of Orthodox Christendom. After the Norman Conquest of England a great synod had been held at Winchester to reform the irregular Anglo-Saxon Church on the strict Roman pattern. After the Norman Conquest of Ireland a great synod was held, under Henry's auspices, at Cashel, to introduce similar reforms into the still more irregular Church of Ireland. By the decrees of that synod the Church, the soul of the world, was liberated from the unclean dominion of the sept. All Church property was freed from the exactions of the chiefs, both in the way of money and entertainment; and clergymen were exempted from paying their share of the Eric, or fine for blood, with the other members of the sept in case of homicide. The payment of tithes was enjoined on all the faithful. The claim of each dead man's soul to a certain part of his chattels after his death was asserted in the interest of the priests by whom the masses for the soul were sung. The ecclesiastical restriction on marriage within the prohibited degrees, and the observance of the rite of baptism to be performed at the consecrated font, were enforced. Finally, it was ordained that all things pertaining to divine worship should for the future throughout Ireland be regulated after the model of Holy Church, according to the observances of the Church of England. The decrees of the synod affected to be made for all Ireland, but their operation was really confined to the part in the power of the Anglo-Normans and under Anglo-Norman law.

This great achievement of the Norman race and of Holy Church woke all the echoes of renown. It was chronicled by Giraldus Cambrensis, preceptor and companion to Prince John in Ireland, in a Latin history, which its vain but talented author, like another Herodotus reading his history at Olympia, recited before the University of Oxford; the recitation occupying three days, and being accompanied by great entertainments to the students and the poor. It was chronicled in a long Norman-French poem by a minstrel who derived his account from Maurice Regan, the interpreter of Dermot. These writers were not Anglo-Saxons, nor was it for the Anglo-Saxons that they wrote. They were Norman chroniclers, and their notes of triumph fell on the ears only of the conquering race.

In the case of England, the Normans completed the conquest; settled over the whole country and formed a landed aristocracy; introduced probably everywhere, at the expense of much misery, a loftier type of character and a higher civilization; gave spirit and purpose to a somewhat dull and aimless race; and in course of time melted down into the mass of the English people. In the case of Ireland, the energy of the conquering race being drawn away by the Crusades, and by the allurements of adventure in the sunnier and more glorious fields of France, they formed only a military colony, or rather a garrison, holding its ground against the natives with difficulty, and living in a perpetual state of border war. Thus at the commencement of the connexion between England and Ireland, the foundation was inevitably laid for the fatal system of Ascendancy; a system under which the dominant party were paid for their services in keeping down rebels by a monopoly of power and emolument, and thereby strongly tempted to take care that there should always be rebels to keep down.

The 'Pale,' of which the history extends from the Conquest to the time of the Tudors, was a fragment of feudal England placed on the other side of the Irish channel. It presented, in a coarse form, all the features of feudal organization and baronial life. It had its counterparts of the Great Charter, and of all the constitutional statutes which the Great Charter drew in its train. It had its royal courts of law; it had its royal judges of assize, though their short circuits round Dublin were compared to the contracted revolution of the Cynosure round the pole; it had its council of barons, though there was not political spirit enough in a distracted and unprosperous community effectually to perform the spontaneous process of developing the council into a regular Parliament with a lower house consisting of representatives of the people. There was, in truth, no people to represent.

But the thing which was most fatal both to the political prosperity of the Pale and to the extension of the English dominion beyond its bounds, was the absence of the king. In the feudal system there were two forces at work, that of the monarchy and that of the aristocracy. The combined action of the two was attended by perpetual jarring and discord between them; but both were necessary to the production of that ordered liberty which we enjoy under the Constitution. The monarchy preserved the principle of government and the common interest of the State; the aristocracy preserved the principle of liberty and the interests of personal independence. Without the monarchy there would have been a Polish anarchy; without the aristocracy there would have been an Oriental despotism. In either case political progress would have been arrested. The Anglo-Irish were practically without a king, and the chronic anarchy of an uncontrolled aristocracy was the inevitable result.

The same circumstance was, if possible, still more injurious to the native race. The Irish were, and long remained, in that stage of political development when an object of personal loyalty, such as a clansman finds in his chief, was essential in order to engage their present allegiance, and train them for a higher form of political life. The talisman of the royal presence has never been tried on their hearts without effect; but that talisman has been too seldom tried. Henry II., John, Richard, James II., and George IV., all were welcomed in a manner which none of them except the first deserved. William III. visited Ireland, but visited it as a party chief and an avenger. The Irish are expected to be loyal; yet it is difficult to imagine how loyalty can be kindled in the heart of a rude clansman or an ignorant peasant who seldom hears of, and never sees, his king.

The adventurers, like the Spanish adventurers in the distant conquests of Spain, soon fell out among themselves; and had not the Irish chiefs been rendered incapable of steady combination by rivalries still more bitter and feuds still more reckless, the strangers would have been driven into the sea. There was no superior authority to unite and direct their scanty forces in the prosecution of their conquest; no one to control their suicidal violence and treachery in their dealings with the natives, to receive the submission of those Irish who were willing to submit, and assure them protection in return; to exhibit that image of stable government, law, and justice, by which civilized conquerors seldom fail to impose upon the minds of a barbarous race, and which has done more perhaps even than our victorious arms, to extend our dominion over the anarchic satrapies of Hindostan.

In other respects, all that was bad in feudalism was at its worst in Ireland. The policy of William the Conqueror had avoided giving large seigniories in one place to any of his barons except the Marchers, whom it was at once necessary and safe to place at the head of a considerable feudal power. In Ireland, this policy could not be observed. It was necessary to grant to each adventurer as much as his sword could win. There were no less than eight counties palatine, each a legalized anarchy, at one time. The King's Peace could scarcely be said to exist, and every baron revelled in the full license of private war.

Sir John Davis has remarked that there were no forests. The wilds were abandoned to outlaws, who in the English forests were in some measure kept under by the forest police, which partly compensated thereby the evils of the forest laws.

It naturally resulted from the nature of the conquest as a private adventure that the castles and fortifications of the conquerors were built, not with a view to commanding the country and keeping down the natives, but with a view to holding the richest plains and valleys for the private benefit of the adventurers. Thus the natural fastnesses of the country remained in the hands of the natives; and the conquest never was consolidated or assured. In some cases the colonists seem to have neglected building castles altogether. The family of Savage in the North were driven out of their possessions by the natives owing to their having acted on the pithy maxim that "a castle of bones was better than a castle of stones."

Even the evil of absenteeism had an early origin in the ill-fated country. The English barons who married the five daughters and shared the vast inheritance of William Earl of Pembroke, lord of all Leinster, had greater estates in England than in Ireland, and managed their Irish estates through seneschals, the middlemen of those days. The drain of rent from a country is the least of the evils of absenteeism: the greatest is the absence of the class which is destined, from its position and intelligence, to be a guide and a source of civilization to the rest.

The Church of the Pale was in like manner an exaggeration of all that was worst in the feudal Church. Its clergy were more secular, its abuses were more rank; it was more incapable of breathing the gentle spirit of Christianity into hard natures, and mitigating the evils of fierce and cruel times. The ministry was polluted at the outset by clerical adventurers, some of them of the fighting kind, who swarmed over from England to a harvest of booty, not of souls. The Prelates were not content with hurling at each other the javelins of excommunication in spiritual fray. One of them besieged a brother bishop in his own cathedral, loaded him with chains, and cast him into a dungeon, from which he barely escaped with life. Another was named Burn-bill or Scorch-villain, because he had burned all the title-deeds of his tenants, after fraudulently getting possession of them, in order that they might thenceforth hold at will. A third is stated, in a petition presented against him, to have starved to death six persons whose inheritance he had got into his hands. From that which was her most obvious work as a Christian Church, and the performance of which could alone justify her existence, the evangelization and civilization of the natives, the Church of the Pale was almost inevitably cut off by the fatal impediment of language, added to the hostile relations between the natives and the inhabitants of the Pale.

It is not surprising to find Pharisaical fanaticism and cruelty linked with Sadducean depravity and worldliness. The Bishops of the Pale were active persecutors of heretics and burners of witches.

In one respect the Irish barons shewed themselves religious; their wild remorse for their wild crimes covered the country with monastic foundations. Near four hundred monasteries were suppressed by Henry VIII., and it was vaguely reckoned that the monks amounted to half the population[t]. In Barrow Bay, where the conquerors first set foot, rose St. Mary of Tintern, a daughter of Tintern-on-the-Wye; and a monastery near Dublin, founded by Henry II., bore the name of the martyr Thomas à Becket. These foundations were not for the native and the suffering, but for the intrusive and the dominant race; they were in part, like the wealthy Protestant Hierarchy of modern times, trophies of the invasion. Yet, like the Abbey

[t] See Mant., vol. i. p. 40.

which the victorious Norman raised to commemorate and sanctify the bloody day of Hastings, and the other foundations of remorseful superstition, they could not fail to be in some degree houses of mercy, and witnesses along the path of conquest to the power which is above the strong. The mere creation of architectural beauty destined for a religious purpose must always have had a humanizing effect, if it had no effect of a more deeply religious kind.

The kings of England, in those days ruling over a turbulent and intriguing aristocracy, could not venture to leave the seat of government. They were compelled to govern Ireland by deputy. But who was to be the deputy? If an Irish baron was chosen, all the other Irish barons would be his rivals. If an English baron was sent, all the Irish barons would be his enemies. There were already in the Pale, as there were afterwards in the days of Swift and Boulter, an English and an Irish interest; the English interest desiring to bind Ireland firmly to England by giving all the preferment to those who had estates in the mother country, the Irish interest contending that the native Anglo-Irish should be alone entitled to the spoil. Ecclesiastics, separated in some degree from baronial interests and factions, yet respected by the barons from the sanctity of their profession, performed a useful function as statesmen in the middle ages, though at some sacrifice of the more immediate objects of their calling. To their order recourse was more than once had for a governor. But ecclesiastics had strong class and corporate interests of their own, which took precedence in their councils of the common weal. The example of the new Hildebrand and glorious martyr Thomas à Becket had at this time helped to stimulate them to the highest pitch of rebellious termagancy and insolent defiance of the lay power. The Irish ecclesiastics formed a confederacy, as anarchic as any confederacy of barons, for the maintenance of their interests and privileges against secular jurisdiction. Nor were they much easier to deal with than rebellious barons because they relied less on men-at-arms, and more on excommunications, anathemas, and an appalling apparatus of crucifixes crowned with thorns and sweating blood.

The project appears to have been formed at one time of making the Lordship of Ireland a sort of appanage of a prince of the blood, and John and Edward I. bore the title of Lord of Ireland under the kings their fathers as Suzerains. The presence of a member of the royal family was a talisman which never failed to work good effects, as the Irish barons themselves had the discernment to see. Even the visit of the worthless John produced some improvements of an important kind in the administration of the Pale.

A deceptive ray of hope gleamed upon the fortunes of the country when Edward I. received the title of its Lord. Had he been able to take up his residence in his appanage and devote his genius as a soldier and a statesman to its affairs, he would perhaps have cut short the tragedy of Irish history. He would have set imperial interests and the interests of the whole people decisively above those of private adventurers, and of a ruling caste. He would have subdued Ireland, as he subdued

Wales, by a comprehensive and effectual plan of operations, such as the barons never attempted to undertake, though they went forth on "hostings," and vainly chased septs, light and disencumbered as the birds of the air, among trackless woods and treacherous bogs. And when Ireland had been subdued, he would have settled it, as he settled Wales, with a due regard at once to the claims of native customs and to the claims of superior civilization, and with as much humanity and wisdom as could find place in the mind of a conqueror in that, or perhaps in any age. But the Prince was first detained in England by civil war, and afterward drawn away to the Crusades; and the only proof of his statesmanship which he gave to Ireland was an attempt to control from a distance the anarchical pretensions of the Churchmen.

In the reign of Edward II. the brilliant Gaveston displayed his military prowess in Irish warfare, and restored for a moment the fortunes of the Pale. But the disastrous war with Scotland brought down Edward Bruce as a competitor for the Irish crown. Some of the most powerful among the native chiefs declared for him. His pretensions were abetted, it seems, by the intrigues of the malcontent ecclesiastics, who thus early in Irish history formed a kind of Repeal party. But Anglo-Norman valour and policy put forth their power in extremity against an ill-cemented league. The Pope, who at first had lent an ear to the representations of the ecclesiastical Dis-unionists, at last interposed with spiritual thunder in support of his predecessor's grant to the English Crown. And Bruce, ill-supported by his passionate and fickle allies, paid the forfeit of his adventurous ambition with his life at the decisive battle of Dundalk, where the valour and conduct of John de Bermingham half effaced the stain of Bannockburn. But the land was left in a state of appalling desolation: and what was perhaps still worse, it had been discovered by the enemies of England that Ireland was the weak point of the English monarchy; and an example had been set of foreign intervention which was destined to be fruitful in calamities without end.

Then followed the wars with France, glorious to England as proofs of her military prowess, but in other respects fatal to both nations. Edward III. and Henry V. took little thought for a barbarous and barren dependency, while they were playing for the most splendid prize of fame and empire. They cared only to draw from it a supply of light infantry, whose knives found their way between the joints of feudal harness on those famous fields where, in the overthrow of the French chivalry by peasant hands, feudalism found its grave. Once indeed, urged by the spirit of a victorious nation, the great Plantagenet monarchy came to the conquest of Ireland with overwhelming power. Thirty thousand of the archers of Crecy and Poictiers disembarked at Dublin to certain victory. But at their head was Richard II. That trifler received only the nominal submission of the chiefs, who bowed their heads like reeds before his presence, and raised them again as lightly when he was gone. The popular administration of Richard Duke of York, in the time of Henry VI., served merely to draw after him the strength of the Pale to perish on the field of

Wakefield. No aid of course could be lent by the Government of England, when it was itself distracted and bankrupt, to the Government of Ireland towards the prosecution of the Conquest. The utmost that could be done was to order Irish absentees to repair to their estates and benefices in Ireland, and recruit the declining numbers of the colony. The government of the Pale was in a state of chronic dissolution. As a last expedient, one lawless faction was played off against another, and a sort of balance of anarchy was kept up by fostering the feuds between the house of Ormond and that of Kildare. The annual financial return from Dublin was *in thesauro nihil*. The troops, left without pay, lived at free quarters on the unhappy colonists, practising every kind of license and of rapine. The Government, like the disorganized Spanish monarchy, was fain to hand over the primary duty of maintaining some sort of police to a private association called the Brotherhood of St. George. At the accession of Henry VII. the English dominion in Ireland was verging upon extinction.

Not only had the Pale failed to gain upon the Irishry, the Irishry had gained greatly by contagion and assimilation on the disorganized Pale. The inhabitants of the island may be almost said to have been constitutionally divided into three classes; "the king's Irish subjects," "the king's Irish rebels," and "the king's Irish enemies." The ranks of the "king's Irish rebels" were mainly recruited from degenerate English, who in a spirit of lawlessness, or more probably to escape the black-rent which the powerful Irish chieftains levied on the inhabitants of the enfeebled Pale, forswore their character as Englishmen; took Irish names; adopted the Irish tongue; let their hair and moustache grow after the wild Irish fashion; put on the wild Irish garb, the great folds of saffron-coloured linen, and the long mantle which was viewed with suspicion by the Government as the garment of all who lay abroad at night; learnt to ride without saddles after the Irish fashion; contracted marriage, fosterage, and gossiprede with the natives; and fell into all the habits of a wild and roving clansman's life. Some of the barons had become chiefs; formed their retainers into bastard septs; exchanged the English for the Brehon law, or rather for the lawless tyranny of a chieftain in his hold; and instead of regular rents and services, learnt to practise the irregular exactions called by the English Coyne and Livery, of which it was said that, though they were invented in Hell, they could not have been practised there, or they would have overturned the kingdom of Beelzebub. The principal of these Anglo-Irish septs were those of the Geraldines and the Butlers, whose deadly feuds rivalled those of genuine clans. An Act of the Irish Parliament was passed to abolish the words Crom-a-boo and Butler-a-Boo, the slogans of these two clans. These renegades to Irishry seem to have imbibed even the peculiarities of Irish intellect: for the Earl of Kildare, the head of the Geraldines, being summoned to answer for having committed an act of sacrilege by burning down the Cathedral of Cashel, pleaded in his defence that he thought the Archbishop was in it.

To arrest this tendency was the object of the Statute of Kilkenny passed under the auspices of Lionel, Duke of Clarence, the Governor of Ireland. There is nothing peculiarly malignant in the attempt of that statute to restore a sharp division between the English and the natives. The object of the framers was not to prevent the beneficial fusion of the two races into one nation, but to prevent the one which they very naturally and rightly thought the more civilized, from degenerating into the barbarism of the other; and at the same time to check the increase of the "rebel" element in the country. The clause forbidding the English to let the Irish graze cattle on their lands has been regarded as a startling instance of inhuman exclusiveness. But the fact probably was that such a community of pasturage would have drawn the Englishman into the Irishman's sept. The same legislators forbid, under the severest penalties, the making of private war on the Irishry, and the exciting them to war. Mr. Hallam has observed that "we shall scarcely find in Irish history during the period of the Plantagenet dynasty that systematic oppression and misrule which is every day imputed to the English nation and its government." The truth is that the Plantagenet government, when it found time to attend to Ireland, intended not evil but good to the Irish people. But its orders, when they were most beneficent, were issued in vain to the fierce and strong-handed feudatories of the distant Pale, yielding but an ironical allegiance to their suzerain, and themselves profiting by and rejoicing in the anarchy which they were enjoined to quell.

It sounds shocking that the killing of an Irishman by an Englishman should have been no felony, and that it should have been a good plea to an indictment for murder that the murdered person was not an Englishman, nor a member of one of the five "bloods" or septs which had been admitted within the pale of the English law. But nothing more is in fact implied in this than that the Irish were not under the English, but under the native or Brehon jurisdiction. The existence of two races in the same country under different laws, and with different punishments for crimes, inconceivable as it appears now, appeared quite natural at a time when the distinction of races was far stronger, and when law was the peculiar custom of the race, not a set of principles common to all mankind. It would have been the same in England had the Anglo-Saxons succeeded in obtaining from the Conqueror "the laws of Edward the Confessor." One kingdom would then have contained two nations, the Normans and the Saxons, living under different penal codes. The rule of impunity held good for both sides alike. An Irishman who had murdered an Englishman would have been only fined for it by his Brehon. The Government having on one occasion desired a native chief to receive a sheriff into his territories, the chief consented, but at the same time desired the Government to say what sum of money, or Eric, they set upon the Sheriff's head, in order that, if he was killed, that sum might be duly assessed upon the sept.

The English Government was not unwilling to admit the Irishry to the English law. Five whole septs, the five bloods (*quinque sanguines*) above alluded to, were admitted collectively; and individual denization seems to have been freely granted. But the Irish barons, through whom the English Government had in the main to act, were not of the same mind. A large body of Irish petitioned for the English law in the reign of Edward I., offering 8,000 marks as a fee for the favour. The king desired that attention might be paid to the petition, though, after the fashion of the needy governments of those times, he wished to sell the grant at as high a price as he could. But the Irish barons evaded his injunctions.

The idea that the English Government deliberately excluded the Irish from the pale of humanity vanishes away. Nevertheless, those who are disposed to regard the Irish as inherently lawless, will do well to remember the historical relations between that people and the English law. Aliens to it for four centuries after the Conquest, they subsequently experienced it not as a beneficent and protecting power, but as an evil mystery of iniquitous technicalities, a cold craft which disinherited them of their lands in a manner at once more systematic and more hateful than the conqueror's sword. Sir John Allen, Master of the Rolls in Ireland, wrote to the Lord Deputy, Sir Anthony St. Leger, and the other Commissioners appointed to report on the state of the country in 1537, that he "had been of this opinion ere now, that the Irish were more conformable to good order than diverse of the King's subjects, and kept their troths better." A people cannot be expected to love and reverence oppression because it is consigned to a Statute-book and called law.

From the ruins of the feudal aristocracy, which the Wars of the Roses had laid in the dust, arose the powerful monarchy of the Tudors. A new order of things commenced. Ireland as well as England began to feel the action of a stronger and more concentrated administration, and one which, the intervening barrier of the nobility being removed, was brought into more immediate contact with the mass of the people.

To complete the subjugation of the dependency, and to bring the whole of it under English law, soon became a leading object with the sovereigns, the statesmen, and the political theorists of the day. The intellect of England, aroused to surpassing activity by the great controversies of the sixteenth century, did not neglect this topic of speculation. The poet Spenser in the reign of Elizabeth, and the cultivated statesman Sir John Davis in the reign of her successor, inquired in elaborate treatises why Ireland had never been conquered; why it remained, in spite of all its resources, a land of perpetual want and misery, and a perpetual drain on the resources of England; and how this evil might be remedied, and this reproach taken away. The same problem engaged, together with the great problems of science, the all-embracing mind of Bacon. In these speculations, the ideal which statesmen and philosophers alike had before their eyes, was the subjugation and settlement of Wales by Edward I.

The grand obstacles to such a subjugation and settlement were the power and independence of the great

Irish chiefs, and especially of those who were at the head of the powerful septs of Geraldine and O'Neil. With these chiefs a long, desperate, and wavering struggle of policy and arms accordingly commenced. It ended in the total overthrow of the chiefs, whose power finally sank in the fall of Tyrone. But it left Ireland a waste of blood and ashes.

Henry VII. was led, both by his temperament and his precarious position, to employ the weapons of policy rather than of force. He governed Ireland for the most part by the hand of the Earl of Kildare, head of the Geraldines, whom he did his best, by favours and caresses, to secure to his interest, and to whose equivocal conduct he was discreetly blind. "All Ireland," said the Council, according to a somewhat apocryphal anecdote, "cannot govern this man." "Then," replied the King, "this man shall govern all Ireland." But phantoms rose in Ireland from the grave of the House of York; and both Simnel and Warbeck found eager support among barons restless by habit as well as from recent civil war, and among a people equally restless, and ever craving for even the shadow of a king. Henry was compelled to take active measures, and Sir Edward Poynings went over as Lord Deputy, armed with the full power of Government, and charged to effect a general reformation. Sir Edward's military efforts were for the most part baffled by the nimbleness and ubiquity of an almost impalpable foe. But his legislative measures produced momentous effects. The most memorable of the Statutes passed by him, and those which made his name so rife in the constitutional controversies of a later period, were the two which assured the dependency of Ireland upon England, by extending the operation of English Statutes to Ireland, and by rendering the previous consent of the English Privy Council necessary to all the Acts of the Irish Parliament [u]. But besides these, he was the author of a large mass of useful enactments, restraining the great lords from harassing the subject by the exaction of coyne and livery; checking the process of persecution and eviction by which they were clearing their territories of English freeholders to fill them with Irish serfs; breaking up their bands of armed retainers; prohibiting their private wars against the Irish; and enforcing against them and other degenerate English the most important of the Statutes of Kilkenny. A determined blow was struck at the besetting evil of factious combination in all forms. And by a most enlightened and praiseworthy provision, the practice of taking a fine from the sept in case of murder was put down, and it was ordered that murderers should in all cases be prosecuted according to the provisions of the English law.

The name of Poynings was a byeword of infamy among the Irish patriots, or to call them by a more appropriate name, the "Irish interest," during the last century. But it can hardly be doubted that the most obnoxious of his statutes, as they tended to make imperial policy and imperial interests paramount over the policy and interests of Ascendancy, were at the time of their enactment beneficial to the Irish people.

[u] Leland, bk. iii. ch. 5.

Aware of the power of personal influence, Henry drew the Irish lords to his court at Greenwich, where they were graciously received, and where those who supported Simnel, as a gentle rebuke, were waited on at table by that pretender. "In the absence of your king," said Henry to them, "you would crown apes." And, in the absence of their king, they will.

Wolsey, the Richelieu of the Tudor era, inspired the policy of Henry VIII. The object of completely incorporating Ireland in the Empire, and assimilating its institutions to those of England, was soon taken up, and was urged forward during the greater part of the reign, both by address and arms. Henry, who saw the barons of England under his feet, was little likely to brook, in his other kingdom, such independence as that of the Irish chief who sent his henchman to beard him in the midst of his court, and demand the punishment of an obnoxious Earl on pain of war. Arms were employed first, under commanders sent from England, and on the whole with success. Then diplomacy took its turn. The great chiefs were drawn to London; peerages were lavished on them; and they were induced to recognise Henry as King of Ireland, a title which he assumed in place of the former title of Lord, in token that a new order of things had commenced; and probably also with a view to assert his right to Ireland independently of the Pope. At the same time, measures were taken by the English governors of Ireland, in whose administration the deep and reflecting statecraft of a politic age now began to appear, to undermine the authority of the chiefs, by detaching from them the allegiance of the members of their septs, and winning the natives from the Brehon to the English law. But the chiefs, with the quick discernment of their race, easily perceived that their destruction as independent potentates was intended. One by one, as the danger approached them, or in loose confederacies, which rivalry and perfidy were always breaking up, they hurled themselves against the power whose toils were closing round them, and filled the succeeding reigns with unquenchable, bloody, and desolating war.

The main struggle, in the Irish wars of Henry VIII., was with the great house of the Geraldines, Earls of Kildare, of whom it was reported in a despatch to Cromwell that "this English Pale, except the towns and very few of the possessioners, be so affectionate to the Geraldines, that for kindred, marriage, fostering, and adhering as followers, they covet more to see a Geraldine reign and triumph, than to see God come among them." The partizans of the family were marked on the breast with a G, in token that they "owed their hearts to the Geraldines." This great house was reduced, in an ill-starred struggle, to a boy, who escaped the fangs of Henry, and became the stock from which the race shot up anew.

The natives fought like savages, as they still were; and the English emulated their savageness. Great atrocities were committed in cold blood on the garrisons of captured strongholds, and the country of the hostile septs was burnt and ravaged with the same merciless barbarity which marked the inroads of the Tudor commanders upon Scotland. The evil and treacherous statecraft which filled the councils of princes in the age of Machiavelli, and from which the lofty mind of Bacon himself was by no means free, gave itself the fullest license in dealing with a race of barbarians remote from the domain even of such public opinion as existed in those times. The Earl of Kildare was induced to surrender himself to the Deputy, Lord Leonard Gray, under a promise of mercy, confirmed, according to one account, by taking the Sacrament. The Government, which was bent on having the Earl's blood, yet embarrassed by the engagements of its representative, solved the difficulty by keeping him for a time in prison, and then putting him to death. With him perished his five uncles, three of whom had been treacherously arrested by the Lord Deputy at a banquet to which he had invited them, and to which they had come without suspicion, being entirely innocent of their nephew's rebellion. One propagator of civilization and true religion among the natives did not scruple when a notable rebel had submitted, to make him give a pledge of his submission by committing an act of foul treachery against his late associates. Another, after a battle gained by the help of Irish auxiliaries, told his victorious countrymen that, to complete their victory, they had only to cut the throats of their allies. Sir John Perrot was the best and most honourable of the Governors of Ireland during the Tudor period. At his departure, the people followed him with tears to the shore. Yet even he did not scruple to kidnap in the foulest manner, and keep as a hostage at Dublin, the son of a chief whose fidelity he had some reason to suspect.

Few will be deluded by the notion that atrocity denotes vigour, or that the want of good faith and humanity among the natives could excuse a want of good faith and humanity among their invaders. In subduing a savage or half-civilized race, it is necessary, no doubt, to maintain the superiority of the civilized nation in arms and the art of war; but it is still more necessary to maintain the superiority of a civilized nation in veracity, justice, and self-command. From the blood of the Geraldines, cruelly and perfidiously shed by Henry VIII., arose the Desmonds and Tyrones, who all but wrested Ireland from Elizabeth. Conquest is at best a questionable process; but it loses its only warrant when the conqueror descends to the barbarism of the conquered.

At no period of the struggle, unhappily, could England put forth her whole power to strike, in mercy, a decisive blow. The service in Ireland was starved throughout the reign of Henry VIII. by that king's reckless wars upon the Continent, and the bankruptcy to which, in spite of his immense confiscations, his finances were reduced. The governments of Protector Somerset and of Mary were distracted by other struggles and perils; and Elizabeth had Spain as well as Ireland on her hands. But the best use was not made even of the forces which were sent. Able men, indeed, were appointed to the command. Bellingham, St. Leger, Sydney, Perrot, and Lord Mountjoy were, as soldiers and statesmen, worthy of an age which, from the union of high intellectual cultivation with habits of action among the higher classes, was singularly fruitful of men suited at once for war and council. But the constant change of governors produced a perpetual oscillation of policy between severity and clemency, force and conciliation, preference for the English and preference for the Irish interest, which was ill-adapted to command the submission of a quick-witted and high-mettled race. "The people of that country," says the author of the Life of Sir John Perrot[x], "are for the most part naturally wise, and able to observe the best advantage and opportunity to obtain their purposes." "The ignorance of the governors," says the same writer[y], "had also sometimes given great advantage to the ill-affected subjects, who being like to colts not well ridden, when they find the rider not to carry a straight even hand and a sure seat, will strive to take the head, and run away with their rider, or to cast him out of his seat if they can." Each governor, during his short period of command, had much to learn, and probably, if he brought with him English notions of administration, much to unlearn. But those who had the will and the power to pursue a steady policy of justice did not fail to experience the correctness of the further remark,—" Yet to say the truth, the people of that country love to be justly dealt withal by their governors, however they deal with one another, and will do more at the command of their governor, whom they repute and have found to be just,

[x] p. 143.   [y] p. 142.

than by the strict execution of the laws or constraint of any force or power."

The beneficent administration of Sir John Perrot was embarrassed and at length overthrown by delation and intrigue. These, curses inherent in the government of dependencies, were ever present to thwart the work of subjugation and settlement. The evil influence of the unscrupulous and sanguinary factions which darkly struggled for ascendancy in the Councils of Henry VIII. was seen in the mysterious fall and death of Lord Leonard Gray. Nor did favouritism fail to play its part. Elizabeth, at the most critical moment of a desperate struggle, gave the command in the Netherlands to the incompetent Leicester, and the command in Ireland to the equally incompetent Essex.

Finally there was corruption; corruption in the very vilest form; corruption which preferred war to peace because war held out hopes of lucre which peace threatened to destroy. The great events and discoveries of the Elizabethan era produced a love of adventure which broke forth in every direction, and varied in the dignity of its objects and in its character, from the height of heroism to the depth of baseness. The eagles took wing for the Spanish main; the vultures descended upon Ireland. A daring use of his sword procured for the adventurer in the Spanish colonies romantic wealth in the shape of ingots and rich bales; a dexterous use of intrigue, chicanery, and the art of inciting to rebellion, procured for the sharper in Ireland wealth less romantic, but more solid and lasting, in the shape of confiscated lands. The appearance of these adventurers, and the commencement of their hateful trade, made the war internecine. Submission may avail with the tyrant but never with the confiscator.

In the beginning of Elizabeth's reign the great rebel chieftain, Shane O'Neil, appeared in London on the wise invitation of the Queen, conveyed through his cousin, the loyalist Earl of Kildare. The chieftain was attended through the streets by a guard of gallow-glass armed with axes, bare-headed, their hair falling in curls, yellow shirts dyed with saffron, long sleeves, short coats and hairy mantles. He marched in this order to the palace, where he was presented to the Queen, and threw himself on his face before her, confessing his rebellion "with howling[z]." His want of courtliness amused the courtiers; but the Queen seems to have exerted her tact and cordiality of manner to win his heart.

But this was only an interlude. The long reign of Elizabeth was, in Ireland, one of incessant war, chiefly against the great rebels, as they were called, John O'Neil, Desmond, and Tyrone. In John O'Neil, who was slain by the foulest treachery, and Desmond, who when an aged and helpless wanderer was cruelly hunted down and butchered, may be said to have perished the last, properly speaking, of the Irish Chiefs; Tyrone was more an English courtier and soldier than an Irish chieftain. In this respect he resembled Owen Glendower, the last leader who raised the standard of independence in Wales. He held his title and estates under an English grant, though it was one which con-

[z] The "Earls of Kildare," by the Marquis of Kildare, p. 204.

firmed the Brehon rule entitling bastards to their share in the succession. He had moved with distinction in the brilliant court of Elizabeth, and his politeness and address appear to have caught the susceptible fancy of the Queen. His military talents were proved by the length and skilfulness of his resistance: and they were aided by the knowledge of character and the dexterity in dealing with men which he had acquired by converse with the great world. Essex, as Lord Lieutenant, commanded against him. Tyrone, well knowing his man, sought a personal conference. The two generals led their armies to the opposite banks of a river, and then rode to a ford. Scarcely had the feet of Essex's charger touched the water, when Tyrone spurred his horse into the stream till the water rose above his saddle, and crossed to the other side to pay his homage to his illustrious opponent. The chivalrous soul of Essex was touched and his vanity flattered by such an act of courtesy and confidence: in the conversation which followed he opened his ear and heart to the wily chieftain, and when the conference ended he was undone.

Tyrone had served the Crown loyally against other rebels, and it does not appear that he would have rebelled himself had he not seen too well that his vast estates were marked by the confiscators for their prey. He received his last warning in the fate of the neighbouring chief McMahon, who was brought to trial, it is said, before a jury of common soldiers, and executed on a technical charge of treason, for having collected his rents after the Irish fashion, with the strong hand;

while the official harpies by whom he had been murdered shared his lands.

Spenser saw the state of Munster after these wars. The people, he says, "were there brought to such wretchedness, as that any stony heart would have rued the same. Out of every corner of the woods and glens they came creeping forth upon their hands, for their legs would not bear them; they looked like anatomies of death, they spake like ghosts crying out of their graves; they did eat the dead carrions, happy where they could find them, yea, and one another soon after, in so much as the very carcasses they spared not to scrape out of their graves; and, if they found a plot of water-cresses or shamrocks, there they flocked as to a feast for the time, yet not able long to continue therewithal; so that in short space there were none almost left, and a most populous and plentiful country suddenly left void of man and beast; yet sure in all that war, there perished not many by the sword, but all by the extremity of famine, which they themselves had wrought."

The famine, let the Lord Deputy's secretary say what he pleases, even supposing the people wasted their own country in self-defence, was caused by the cruel war. Another power of evil of the most deadly kind had now appeared in full force upon the scene. The ferocity and the horrors of civil war had been increased by foreign intervention. Ireland had at last been fairly drawn into the spreading vortex of the great religious war which raged for a century between the Catholic and Protestant powers, and carried blood and desolation not into Irish homes alone but into the homes of all Christendom. Previous to the wars of Elizabeth, perhaps, religion had not much to do with Irish insurrections. The decrees of the Romanizing synod of Cashel having remained almost inoperative beyond the Pale [a], the Church of the native Irish septs still retained much of its irregular and isolated character, and was far from being peculiarly under the influence of Rome. The chiefs seem to have paid little attention to the English or Anglo-Irish Reformation. They recognised Henry VIII. with perfect facility, not only as King of Ireland, but as Supreme Head of the Irish Church; and they would probably have recognised him with equal facility as Caliph or as Grand Llama. Even so late as the reign of Elizabeth it was thought that Desmond would have been willing, for the security of his estates, not only to submit to the jurisdiction but to embrace the religion of the Crown. The Pope was anxious to dub Tyrone the champion of the Holy See in Ireland. He sent him, with his benediction, a plume of phœnix feathers, not the last gift of the kind which Ireland has received from the sympathy of foreign liberators. But Tyrone, who had shone at a Protestant court, appears to have been a man of the world, and very indifferent about these things. "Hang thee," said Essex to him, "thou talkest of a free exercise of religion; thou carest as little for religion as my horse." The encroachments of the colony on the native chiefs, and the resistance of the native chiefs to the colony, went on during the reign of Mary as well as during

[a] Lanigan's Eccles. Hist., vol. iv. p. 207.

the reign of Edward VI.; and the names of King's County and Queen's County borne by the territory conquered in the time of that Queen and her husband, are memorials of the fact that the policy of the Catholic Reaction as regarded Ireland was that of other English governments interested in the prosecution of the conquest. After the final rupture between the Crown of England and the Papacy, which took place at the commencement of Elizabeth's reign, and the publication by the Pope of the sentence of excommunication and deposition against the Queen, severer measures began to be adopted against Popish recusants in both kingdoms; and before long Jesuits and seminary priests thrown into Ireland, mingled by their intriguing activity the spirit of religious with that of territorial war. At the same time a Catholic Episcopate, appointed by the Pope, was organized in opposition to that of the Reformed Church, and every effort was made to give the Papal Church in Ireland a distinct existence, to inspire it with a martyr spirit, and prevent it from bowing the knee to Baal. And in truth it soon gave names to the same list of sufferers for conscience' sake which holds the names of Cranmer, Latimer, and Ridley. Yet race and political interest outweighed religious party. Catholics of the Pale were freely employed in the Royal armies, and actively exerted themselves against the armies of Catholic Spain. That violent Ultramontanism which absorbs all the duties and interests of the citizen in those of the Roman devotee, was, like Jesuitism, the peculiar offspring of the great struggle in which the world was now beginning to be involved: it had scarcely been found among ecclesiastics, and never among laymen, in the Catholic communities of the Middle Ages. Like the persecuting spirit of the Crusaders, the terrorism of the Jacobins, and the Protestant fanaticism of the Orange faction, it was a moral epidemic produced by the accidents of a particular crisis in history, and destined, like all such epidemics, ultimately to pass away.

The chiefs were fighting for their lands and power rather than crusading for the faith: but they were not on that account the less ready to accept the aid of Spanish crusaders in their struggle. Of the Armada, which was to sweep the English heretics from the earth, and burst the bonds of the Irish Catholics, Ireland saw only a miserable wreck driven on her coast, where the name of Port-na-Spanien remains a monument of its fate. But twice Spanish expeditions landed and entrenched themselves; first at Smerwick, and afterwards in greater force under Don Juan d'Aquila, at Kinsale, not far from the point afterwards threatened by the invading army of Hoche. The garrison of Smerwick having been forced to surrender at discretion, were butchered in cold blood by order of the Lord Deputy Grey; and Raleigh's name is stained by his having taken part in this detestable service. The act was atrocious, and if, like most writers of Irish history, we keep our eyes fixed on Ireland alone, it will seem without excuse. It will seem atrocious, but not without excuse, if we extend our view, and remember that the conduct of the Spaniards towards the Protestants in the Netherlands was not so much that of cruel men as of fiends, and that they had done all that it was possible to do to put themselves out of the pale of mercy. Elizabeth, however, vindicated English humanity by shewing high displeasure on the occasion. The Irish found the haughty Spaniards far from congenial allies. The Invincibles when foiled loudly laid the blame on their confederates, and D'Aquila, according to Bacon[b], said in open treaty, "that when the devil upon the Mount did shew Christ all the kingdoms of the earth and the glory of them, he did not doubt but the devil left out Ireland and kept it for himself."

The expenses of maintaining the Irish war in Elizabeth's reign were enormous, and went to the heart of the parsimonious Queen. They amounted at last to the annual sum of four or five hundred thousand pounds. The Government was driven to the wretched expedient of debasing the coin, a device by which sharpers were enriched, and the troops disgusted and sent home beggars. Assuredly whoever may have profited by the misery and depression of Ireland, it has not been the English nation. To the English nation Ireland has been a source of expense, danger, and weakness without intermission from the Conquest almost down to the present hour. Sharpers and jobbers may have profited by Irish confiscations and Irish pension lists. But in their profits their country had no part, while its taxpayers were burdened to supply forces for the support of their oppressions, and its existence was imperilled by the invasions which their tyranny provoked. Perhaps there have been few dependencies of which the same

[b] In his treatise "Of a War with Spain."

account might not be rendered if the dominant nation could learn to distinguish between its substantial interest and the gratification of its pride.

It would be absurd to charge the Tudor Government, arbitrary and high-handed as it was, with designs of exterminating or even of depressing the Irish people, though evil thoughts of that kind may sometimes have crossed evil minds. The object of the Government was to pacify and civilize the nation, and to bring it to what in those Councils was of course supposed to be the only true and good religion. Orders were sent to restore the churches, ruined by the spoliations of Henry VIII. and by the ensuing civil wars. Orders were sent to set up free-schools in every parish. Trinity College was founded and endowed on the model of the Colleges at the English Universities, and in the hope that it would become the image of their greatness. The Elizabethan statesmen proved themselves desirous of imparting to Ireland a full measure of the new religious and intellectual life which England was then feeling through every vein. But religious and intellectual life is not to be imparted in this fashion. It must have its source in the heart and mind of the nation.

Trinity College itself held its ground and grew wealthy only to deserve the name of the "Silent Sister;" while its great endowments served effectually to indemnify it against the necessity of conforming to the conditions under which alone its existence could be useful to the whole nation. The Irish intellect appears to possess among other endowments common to it and the French, a remarkable ingenuity in the solution of mathematical problems. It had shewn, in very early times, an aptitude for cultivating the forms of language similar to that which the French possess, and which has made French to some extent the common tongue of educated Europe. But neither these gifts nor any other intellectual gifts of the people were ever brought into play. The native mind found no means of education, and no organs of expression. A double darkness succeeded to the brilliancy of its early light. The want of the "intellectual part" which Spenser noticed in Irish civilization was not supplied: and those momentous influences which the intellectual part of civilization includes, never touched with their beneficent power the moral, social, or religious character of this ill-starred people.

Even the intellectual part of civilization is exceeded in importance by the civilizing influence of religion. The fatal course of events was now complete which was to make the religion of Ireland for centuries to come the bane of her civilization. For by this time the Protestant Church of the State and the Roman Catholic Church of the people had finally assumed the distinct shape of rival communities, arrayed against each other in a hostility so bitter, so inveterate, so intensified by national and political hatred, that it seems destined to pass away only in the general reconciliation of divided Christendom. This had been gradually brought about by a variety of agencies, seconding and enforcing the exhortations and the threats of Rome; by the sedulous and devoted activity of the new monastic order which the endangered Papacy had called to its aid against rising heresy in the sixteenth, as it had done in the twelfth century; by the rebellions and civil wars in which, though, as was before mentioned, they were rather territorial than religious, Roman Catholics were, in the main, arrayed on one side and Protestants on the other; by the close connexion formed with Spain and Philip II. during the insurrection of Tyrone; and, let it not be forgotten, by the pressure of the laws against recusants, which had at first been very loosely executed, but which were more severely enforced in proportion as the English Government was more endangered by the plots of the seminary priests and the arms of Spain. It has been noticed that the line of hostile demarcation between the two religious parties was not drawn among the laity for some time after the Reformation. The same thing may be said to some extent even of the two hierarchies. The Bishops of Clogher and Raphoe, professed Roman Catholics, sat in a parliament called in the middle of Elizabeth's reign by the popular deputy Sir John Perrot. Even in the two succeeding reigns there still remained a middle party, that of the Catholic lords of the Pale, who, though they had set the Acts of Supremacy and Uniformity, like other Acts of Parliament, at defiance, continued to belong rather to the English interest than to that of the Catholic Church. The spirit of confessors and martyrs was, in truth, not likely to be of rapid growth among a body so firmly rooted in the interests of this world as the oligarchy of the Pale.

A singular revolution had thus taken place. The

Church of the Pale, which was originally Roman, had, from the course of political events, become Protestant, though it remained the Church of the Pale; the Church of the people, originally not Roman, became of all the Churches of Europe the most devoted to Rome, though it remained the Church of the people. Thus the determining force in Irish history has been race rather than religion. The difference of religion has been decided, and even inverted, by circumstances connected with the difference of race.

Each Church has been tainted and greatly weakened in the performance of its spiritual duty by political connexion. It has been the unhappy lot of the Irish people never to see the face of religion unpolluted by tyranny, faction, and intrigue. Thrown entirely upon Rome and the Catholic monarchies for protection against persecution, the Irish Catholic Church could not fail to become the most Ultramontane of Churches, and to present to the Protestants the exasperating aspect of a foreign power planted in our nation and ready at any moment to conspire with its foreign allies and patrons for our overthrow. On the other hand the Church of the oppressor, whatever might be the purity of its creed, could not fail to be an object of burning hatred to the oppressed.

Considering the circumstances in which the State Church of Ireland has been placed; considering that it depended for existence, not on the moral allegiance of the people, but upon the support of a political power, of which it necessarily became the servile instrument; it would indeed have needed an extraordinary outpouring of personal graces upon its members to save it from being the least fruitful and the least illustrious of all the Churches of Christendom. It has had among its clergy learned men, such as Ussher, and holy lives, such as that of Bedell. It has endeavoured from time to time, though with little energy and little hope, to carry forward its appointed work, the conversion of the Irish people. It may plead that, in that work, it has had desperate difficulties of special kinds to contend with: the political hostility of the races; the difference of language; the abuse of patronage, which often employed its bishoprics and livings as political bribes, or as lucrative banishments for not the best of the clergy of the English Church; a ritual cold, tedious, and formal, suited perhaps to the sober Saxon, but wholly unsuited to the ardent Kelt. But the grand and apparently insuperable difficulty with which it has had to contend is in effect this, that Christianity cannot be propagated through unchristian institutions, and that the State Church of a dominant minority is an institution which, being unjust, must be unchristian.

Yet the State Church of Ireland, however anomalous and even scandalous its position may be as the Church of a dominant minority upheld by force in the midst of a hostile people, does not, in truth, rest on a principle different from that of other State Churches. To justify the existence of any State Church, it must be assumed as an axiom that the State is the judge of religious truth, and that it is bound to impose upon its subjects, or at least to require them as a community to maintain, the religion which it judges to be true. And such was the opinion of universal Christendom, doubted, if at all, only by a few obscure and contemptible sectaries, at the time when the English Government did in Ireland that which now seems so unreasonable and so unjust. Elizabeth would have appeared, not only to herself but to the most enlightened and liberal men of her age, to be neglecting her paramount duty, had she failed to establish and enforce by at least moderate penalties, in the dependent kingdom, the religion which her wisdom and the wisdom of Parliament had established in her own. When the Catholics writhe under this wrong, let them turn their eyes to the history of Catholic countries, and remember that while the Catholic Church was stripped of her endowments and doomed to political degradation by Protestant persecutors in Ireland, the Protestant Churches were exterminated with fire and sword by Catholic persecutors in France, Austria, Flanders, Italy, and Spain. They may thus learn to judge of past events and of their present position reasonably and charitably, without renouncing for the future their claims to justice.

As to the Catholic Church of Ireland, it has been already pointed out how the circumstances of its origin gave it from the outset an unfortunate bias towards extreme Ultramontanism, and thus made it, as all who are not Ultramontanes would say, a bad instrument for the religious education of the people. It was, of necessity, a peasant Church, and as a peasant Church has, inevitably, been somewhat wanting in learning and refinement. These are defects with which those who have seized its revenues, and impeded by penal laws the education of its clergy, are not in a position to reproach it.

As the Church of the oppressed race, it has naturally become the organ of their grievances, and has been somewhat degraded, as any Church must be degraded, by clerical demagogism and agitation. It has also failed, from the nature of its spiritual system, to cultivate the religious intellect of its members and to teach them the love of reason and of truth, as distinguished from the emotional parts of religion. But its priests have shared and consoled with zeal and constancy the sufferings of the people. They have retained the allegiance of their flocks, partly, no doubt, by what Protestants cannot forbear from holding to be superstition and spiritual intimidation, but principally by worthier means. The general purity of their lives in recent times has been beyond dispute: and in their brief moments of partial ascendancy during successful insurrections, some of them at least have shewn that persecution had taught them mercy. They have, in fact, displayed the virtues of a free Church dignified by suffering. They have seen the sumptucus establishment of France, once perhaps the object of their envy, grow corrupt through wealth and power, and, sapped by infidelity and atheism, fall prostrate before a revolution of which its vices were a principal cause; while their own Church remains rooted in the affections of the people, and maintained almost in splendour by their devotion, in the midst of their misery and want. The Papacy, in its extremity, finds coldness and indifference among the great Catholic nations, where its faith has been supported by immense endowments and upheld by persecuting laws; it finds loyalty and enthusiasm in Ireland, where it has stood by free allegiance alone. In the time of Henry VIII. a prophecy went abroad that the Catholic Church would fall when Ireland ceased to be Catholic. This prophecy, as it coincides with the natural tendency of things, stands a fair chance of being fulfilled. That the affection which is unbought and uncompelled is likely to live the longest, all will admit: while Protestants and philosophers will aver that those who are the farthest from the Papacy may well be expected to love it best. The chill of death is gathering round the heart of the great Theocracy; but the pulses of life still beat strongly in the extremities of its frame, and nowhere more strongly than in Ireland.

James I. found Ireland, after the submission of Tyrone, pacified, in the conqueror's sense, and waiting to be settled. He made an effort, which was sincere, at least, if not very well directed, to do his part. Though his weaknesses have doomed him to be the butt of historians, he must be allowed to have had something of the largeness of view and of the intellectual interest in improvement, which mark cultivated men: and he communed with the philosophic spirit of Bacon. His deputy, Sir Arthur Chichester, seems to have been an able and right-minded statesman; and in Sir John Davis, he had a sagacious and honest adviser, well-intentioned towards the Irish people, though somewhat narrowly English in his plans for their regeneration.

The reign began well, with a broad act of oblivion. Even the arch-rebel Tyrone was received into favour; and the officers of Elizabeth, who had "laboured after that knave's destruction," and "eaten horseflesh in Munster" in toiling to "quell him," were filled with chagrin at seeing him "honoured," "well-liked," and "smiling in peace at those who did hazard their lives to destroy him." The king having given this earnest of his intentions, next proceeded to complete a work which had been greatly advanced under Elizabeth, by reducing the whole of Ireland to shire land, and extending to it, formally at least, the operation of English law, English police, and the principles of English local administration. The civilizing effect of county meetings at assizes, and on other local occasions, was not left out of sight. A judgment of the King's Bench, amounting to a legislative measure, swept away the whole of the Brehon tenures of land, with the relations between chieftain and clansman which they involved; and substituted for them the English tenure of land, with primogeniture, and the regular relations between landlord and tenant. The chiefs gained a boon by having their demesne lands and their territorial rights finally made hereditary instead of elective; while the Government naturally regarded the English as the only civilized and lawful tenure, and deemed that the grand object of all Irish policy was accomplished by transferring the allegiance of the clansman from the chieftain to the law.

There seems no reason to doubt that it was in honest pursuance of the same policy of civilizing and conciliating the Irish, by giving them English institutions, that a Parliament more regular and comprehensive than any which had preceded, was called for all Ireland, without distinction of race or religion. It is true that the Government took active measures to obtain a majority, and that it created a number of rotten, or rather of sham boroughs. But it does not seem that freedom of election was otherwise interfered with; and an electioneering contest of the most genuine kind ensued. The struggle was carried on over the whole country with a spirit worthy of Limerick or Tipperary in the present day, and its result gave the Catholics, not indeed a majority, as they had hoped, but a powerful minority in the House of Commons.

The measure may perhaps be open to criticism on another ground, as having been rather of a Laputan description, and a little too similar to the elaborate constitution, furnished with all the most recent improvements in the way of political orders, divisions, checks, and balances of power, which at a later period the benign wisdom of Locke framed for the backwoodsmen of Carolina. It was necessary to create sham boroughs, not only to give the Government a majority, but because real boroughs there were none; and to many of the Irish constituencies the elective franchise must have been a boon about as welcome and appropriate as it would have been to a tribe of Red Indians. An honest, able, and humane Lord Deputy, with full powers, would probably have done more at that moment than the largest measure of Parliamentary liberty for the pacification and civilization of the country.

Religious division, however, was fatal at the outset to political union and co-operation. The Catholics, on the death of Elizabeth, inflamed by some vague hope of James's favourable inclinations, or excited by the mere prospect of change, had suddenly taken the offensive, and attempted to re-establish their religion by force. Affronted by this insubordination, and pressed by the Puritans, who were now becoming powerful in the English Parliament, the king had begun to execute with more severity the laws against Popish recusants; and matters were made worse by the Gunpowder Plot, in which the fanatics of the Roman Catholic Church gave, as they have too often given, the lie to the professions of loyalty and regard for civil duty sincerely made by her right-minded and moderate members. The power of the great chiefs having been broken, the Catholic interest in Ireland was now led by the priests, exasperated by the oppression of their Church, and the lawyers, who smarted under the oath of supremacy. The two parties met in Parliament burning with mutual hatred. Their fury broke out at once on the election of a Speaker. The Protestant majority went out of the House, according to the usual form, in the division. While they were gone, the Catholic minority elected a Speaker of their own, and placed him in the chair. The Protestants returned and seated their Speaker by force in the Catholic Speaker's lap. The session exploded in a storm of rage and mutual vituperation. Thus auspiciously commenced the history of the real Irish Parliament. A Catholic deputation carried the complaints of the party to the foot of a gracious throne, and were sharply reprimanded for not being happy under the best of all possible administrations. "Did they expect that the kingdom of Ireland should be like the kingdom of Heaven?" The expenses of this deputation were defrayed by a general contribution imposed by moral force on all the members of the Catholic party; and thus was collected the first political rent. The trade of agitation had begun.

But religious divisions, though they overturned the Parliament, were not the main cause of the frightful disasters which soon ensued. The main cause of those disasters was a struggle for land. The discovery and colonization of the new world had produced a rage for "plantations," together with a taste for the Utopian legislation of which new communities are imagined to be the best, though in reality they are the very worst subjects. It is not improbable that the Roman system of colonization, as an instrument for holding in subjection and civilizing conquered countries, may have been present to the minds of Elizabethan statesmen, who were well read in the Classics, and one of the most learned of whom, Sir Thomas Smith, was a leading promoter of the first English plantation in Ireland. These enterprises commenced in the reign of Elizabeth. The first colony was planted in Down and Antrim on lands which were "presumed in law to be vacant" by the attainder of the chieftain O'Neil. The expedition failed of success; "the native occupants," says Hallam, "not acquiescing in this doctrine of our lawyers." A larger colony was afterwards planted with more success in Cork and Kerry. Raleigh embarked in these ventures as he embarked in all the ventures, maritime, military, political, commercial, and literary, of that enterprising time. Spenser was among the Munster colonists. Part of the "Faery Queen" was written at a house on the vineyard of some Irish Naboth; and the subject of that great Protestant allegory was no doubt partly suggested by the territorial antagonism into which its author was brought as a votary of Una with the followers of the false and dispossessed Duessa. The Lord Deputy Grey is Arthegal, the representative of justice in the allegory, attended by Talus with his iron flail; "which indeed," says Hallam, "was unsparingly employed to crush rebellion." Spenser's views for the subjugation of Ireland are somewhat imbued with the vigour of his Arthegal. He seems to revel in the idea of making campaigns against the Irish kern in winter, "when the aire is sharpe and bitter to blow thorough his naked sides and legges." Famine is an instrument of pacification from the use of which he does not recoil. In our own day sentimental writers have been prone to prescribe measures of vigour for the suppressed vices of the Irish character; while statesmen devoid of sentiment have successfully treated the case by the milder method of good government and justice.

James carried on the colonization of Ireland on a greater scale. Immense territories in Ulster forfeited by Tyrone and Tyrconnell were shared among adventurers partly English and partly Scotch, under a somewhat visionary set of regulations, designed to inculcate prosperity and civilization. The adventurers were pretty sure to be for the most part the least gentle and not the most respectable members of the classes and communities from which they came. They diffused civilization among the natives much as an American settler would diffuse it among Red Indians, by improving them, as far as they could, from off the face of the earth. Their fortified houses, or bawns, are the monuments of the relations in which they lived with the surrounding population. The settlement of the Scotch Presbyterians in the North brought another element of confusion into the already boiling and overflowing cauldron of ecclesiastical discord. The attempt to insert civilization into a nation from without, again proved a failure; but the English and Scotch in the Northern settlement formed a vigorous, industrious, and prosperous community of their own. Among the plantation lands which were best cultivated, and became most thickly peopled, were those taken by the city of London, which thus did something to prove that, as far as agriculture is concerned, estates may be well managed by absentees.

It appears, to say the least, extremely doubtful whether the lands of Tyrone and Tyrconnell, on which the Ulster colony was planted, had been forfeited for any real offence, and whether the plot in which those noblemen were alleged to have engaged, was not invented by the teeming brain of officials desirous of sharing their estates. They fled, it is true, but not from justice; for justice, when the forfeiture of land was in prospect, there was none. Spies were set to work to scent out plots, and find matter for charges of treason. Tyrone complained that he was so beset by them that he could not drink a full cup of sack without being delated to the Government. But there was a further question respecting these estates. When the chieftains of the septs O'More and O'Connell were attainted, in the reign of Mary, the septs pleaded that the chieftain could not by his attainder forfeit the sept land, which he had never possessed. It would, perhaps, have been difficult, at that time, in the case of any of the great forfeitures, to meet this plea. A feeling that the land was still theirs, and that they were unjustly kept out of their possessions, seems long to have survived these vast confiscations in the minds of the native proprietors; and perhaps it is not extinct even at the present day. The existing settlement of land in Ireland, whether dating from the confiscations of the Stuarts, or from those of Cromwell, rests on a proscription three or four times as long as that on which the settlement of land rests over a considerable part of France. It may therefore be considered as placed beyond discussion in the estimation of all sane men; and, this being the case, it is safe to observe that no inherent want of respect for property is shewn by the Irish people if a proprietorship which had its origin within historical memory in flagrant wrong, is less sacred in their eyes than it would be if it had its origin in immemorial right.

The disinheritance of the ancient race was carried on not only by high-handed violence, but by a system, which became a trade, of the meanest and most infamous chicane. A set of miscreants called Discoverers made it their business to spy out technical flaws in titles to land, in order that the estates might be judged to escheat to the Crown, from which grants of them were afterwards obtained, in many instances, by the informers or their employers. When property had recently been unsettled by long civil wars or numerous forfeitures, and when the legal tenure of all the land in the country had just been changed, there were inevitably plenty of openings for enterprises of this kind. "Under pretence," says Carte, speaking of these adventurers, "of improving the King's revenue in a country where it was far less than the charge of government, they obtained commissions of inquiry into defective titles, and grants of concealed lands and rents belonging to the Crown; the great benefit of which was generally to accrue to the projector, whilst the King was contented with an inconsiderable proportion of the concealment, or a small advance of rent. Discoverers were everywhere busily employed in finding out flaws in men's titles to their estates. The old pipe-rolls were searched to find the original rents with which they had been charged; the patent rolls in the Tower of London were ransacked for the ancient grants; no means of industry or devices of craft were left untried to force the possessors to accept of new grants at an advanced rent [c]." It is not surprising that in these cases, again, "the native occupants" should "not have acquiesced in the doctrine of our lawyers." Submit for the present they did. For they had been vanquished in the appeal to force. And if they were tempted to try their right in the courts of law, they found judges who were ministers of iniquity, and juries who gave their verdict, in cases where the

[c] Life of Ormond, bk. i. See also Leland, bk. iv. ch. 8.

Crown was a party, with the terrors of the Star Chamber hanging over their heads.

"In the manuscripts of Bishop Sterne," (in Trinity College,) says Leland, "we find that in the small county of Longford, twenty-five of one sept were all deprived of their estates, without the least compensation, or any means of subsistence assigned to them." This appears to have been one of a number of cases in which the commissioners appointed to distribute the plantation lands had abused their trust, by wresting from the natives the lands, which the King, in marking out the plantations, had reserved for them; and it shews that the offence of the English Government sometimes consisted not in authorizing rapine, but in trusting rapacious hands which it could not control.

In the cathedral of St. Patrick is a sumptuous tomb, which usurped the place of the altar, till the Anglican Strafford indignantly thrust it into a less holy place, and by so doing made a mortal enemy of the wealthy and powerful magnate who had erected it for himself and his descendants. There, in all the honour that can attend the ashes of the great and good, and in more honour than the great and good ever design for their own ashes, lies Richard Boyle, the first Earl of Cork, a penniless London adventurer, who "made Providence his inheritance," and found the hand of Providence most visible in the market of Irish land. In that prosperous trade he throve enormously, became the possessor of vast estates, and of a peerage, and left in Ireland a famous name, which in the hour of his prosperity he did much to deserve, by becoming the best of landlords, and the first of improvers, as well as the father of an illustrious son, and the founder of an honourable line.

The case of the Byrnes of Wicklow, as stated by Carte[d], was one in which, when chicanery had failed, worse instruments were employed to oust innocent men from their rightful inheritance. A criminal prosecution was commenced against the brothers on fictitious grounds by Sir William Parsons and his accomplice in this infamous transaction; and evidence in support of the prosecution was not only raked up from most tainted sources, but wrung out by the use of atrocious tortures, a reluctant witness being placed naked on a burning gridiron, and put to the strappado. The Byrnes were at last released from prison by a commission sent over by the English Government, which had at first been hood-winked, to inquire into the affair: but their lands were never restored to them. Surely these men and their descendants, even to the tenth generation, might be acquitted of inherent depravity if they required Coercion Acts to make them love Sir William Parsons' law.

Security for their lands against the rapacious encroachments carried on in the name of the Crown was the main object of the "graces" which the Catholic nobility and gentry offered to purchase for a large sum of Charles I.; though they sought by the same petition some indulgence for their religion and a redress of the gross abuses which in Ireland as in England disgraced the government, the fiscal system, and the administration of justice. The abolition of the fines exacted for

[d] Life of Ormond, bk. i. p. 74, fol. ed.

ploughing with the tails of cattle, which like the fines for recusancy had turned into a mere harvest for officials, figures strangely in a document analogous to the English Petition of Right. Charles was himself in this transaction. He pocketed the money of the petitioners and then took advantage of a technical breach of Poynings' Law, requiring the previous consent of the English Privy Council to Irish Acts of Parliament, to withhold the capital 'grace' concerning the quieting of titles to land. The door of hope was thus closed against the Irish proprietors, but the course of events soon gave an opening to their despair.

In the meantime Ireland cowered before the imposing but malignant presence of Strafford. That great conspirator clearly regarded the dependent kingdom as a fulcrum on which he might rest the lever that should heave the foundations of English liberty from their place. There an army might be formed which would be entirely at the service of the Crown; and here money might be raised for the purposes of the great enterprise by means of a submissive parliament. For a parliament absolutely submissive to the Crown rather than naked despotism was the political ideal of the Lord Lieutenant's commanding mind, whatever may have been the ideal of the feeble Charles or his foolish and petulant Queen. The Irish Church, too, was to be remodelled according to the theories of Strafford's fellow-conspirator, Laud; and Bramhall, an inferior counterpart of Laud, came over to cast out the spirit of Ussher, as Laud had cast out the spirit of Abbot. Ireland was in Strafford's eyes a conquered country, to be dealt with at the plea-

sure of the conqueror; and he forgot that when rulers
allege a title by conquest they give their subjects an
equal title whenever they have the power to cast off the
conqueror's yoke. His dominion, while he remained
Lord Lieutenant, was absolute. Nor was it altogether
badly used. He would suffer none to commit wrong but
himself. He repressed the license of the soldiery. He
restored the finances; and though, in the supposed interest of England, he iniquitously crushed the Irish
woollen trade, the Irish linen trade regards him as its
founder. The resources of the country rose buoyantly
beneath his master hand: the value of land was increased, shipping multiplied, and if his government had
not been tainted by a sinister object, he would have
proved decisively that the temporary rule of a beneficent despot was the remedy required by the maladies
of the country. But his government was tainted by a
most sinister object, in the pursuit of which he carried
forward on a scale worthy of his greatness as a power of
evil, the legal confiscation of land. The whole province
of Connaught was marked out for spoliation by his
majestic rapine; the pretext being that when the lands
of that province had been surrendered to the Crown and
re-granted, the grants had not been formally enrolled,
though a large sum had been paid in fees for their enrolment. Nor did he confine his aggressions to native proprietors or to feeble victims. On pretence of a technical breach of covenants committed by the colonists of
Londonderry he wrung a great sum from the colony,
and thereby brought down upon his own head and that
of his master the fatal wrath of the mother city, whose

inflexible constancy, power, and wealth, decided the issue of the Civil War.

The Irish Parliament, which had cowered at Strafford's voice when he was present and powerful, turned to rend him when he had been recalled and was struggling for his life. The Revolution had now set in. Its agitating impulse spread first to the Puritans of the colony, who at once arrayed themselves on the side of the Parliament. Then the hearts of the Irish Catholics began to beat thick with the hope of change. The diplomatic craft of Richelieu, the father of all French diplomacy, was sedulously excited to fan the kindling flame of civil war in Ireland, as well as in the other two kingdoms. Rome began to work on the excited mass through her Jesuits and friars. Irish officers dropped in from the armies of France and Spain. Sir Phelim O'Neil and Roger Moore brought with them from exile the influence of the ancient chieftains, the memory of their wrongs, and, what is always indispensable to Irish movements, the talisman of well-known names. Just as the Revolution in England was advancing towards its crisis, and while its leaders were meditating the Grand Remonstrance, the war of the Catholic Confederates commenced with that great massacre of the Protestants in Ulster which is connected with the name of Sir Phelim O'Neil. To doubt that there was a great massacre seems idle, since Clarendon, a contemporary, well-informed, and sober writer, reckoned the number of persons killed at forty or fifty thousand. It seems not less idle to doubt which party struck the first blow: as well might it be doubted which party struck the first blow in the Sicilian Vespers. An abstract of depositions describing some of the scenes which occurred in the massacre has been preserved by Rushworth[e]. It presents an appalling but perfectly credible picture of the vengeance which a people brutalized by oppression wreaks, in the moment of its brief triumph, on the oppressor. Well might phantoms of horror haunt the accursed spots, and the ghosts of the murdered be heard to shriek from beneath the bridge at Portnadown. This outbreak of savage vengeance, however, seems to have been unpremeditated, and opposed to the policy of the leaders, whose design was to expel the Protestants, as the Spaniards had expelled the Moors from Spain, but not to shed their blood. The process of expulsion, executed by the hands of men maddened by such wrongs as those of the dispossessed septmen of Longford or the O'Byrnes, could not fail to lead to bloodshed; and blood once shed, massacre ensued. As soon as the diabolical struggle had begun, the English and Scotch colonists perhaps exceeded the Irish in atrocity, especially when we consider their comparative civilization. The Irish population of Island Magee, though innocent of the rebellion, were massacred, man, woman, and child, by the Scotch garrison of Carrickfergus. The Protestant historian Borlase, a kinsman of the Lord Justice of that name, triumphantly recounting the exploits performed by different regiments against the rebels, tells us that he cannot give the services of each regiment in detail, but that he will give us a specimen, and leave us, as it

[e] Collections, vol. iv. p. 405.

were, to measure Hercules by his foot. He then presents us with a catalogue of the services performed by Sir W. Cole's regiment, one item of which is "starved and famished of the vulgar sort, whose goods were seized on by this regiment, seven thousand¹." Such is the effect of ascendancy on the character of the ascendant party. In England, meantime, the civil war was conducted on the whole, and for that age, with remarkable humanity.

One rainbow appeared amidst this storm to promise that Ireland should not always be drowned in the deluge of hatred. The Evangelical virtues of the Protestant Bishop Bedell protected him, and those who took refuge with him, from the rage of the Catholics in the midst of an internecine struggle. He was made a prisoner, but was treated with respect and humanity by his captors; and when he died, the Irish army buried him with military honours, and joined in the prayer over his grave, *Requiescat in pace ultimus Anglorum.* It was a testimony to the essential identity of the Christian character under the different forms of the two antagonist religions, and a pledge that, in spite of these fratricidal contests, the time would come when the sense of that identity should prevail.

A period of weltering confusion ensued. While the wavering struggle between the King and the Parliament was going on in England, four factions, like four vipers twining together in inextricable entanglements, fought, conspired, and intrigued in Ireland; the Catholic confederates, the Catholic nobility of the Pale, the Protestant royalists, and the Parliamentarians. The

¹ Borlase, p. 87.

Parliamentarians again, in Ireland as well as in England, split among themselves, as the Revolution advanced, into two parties,—that of the Presbyterians, who were for King and Covenant, and that of the Independents, who were for an uncovenanted republic. The Catholic nobility of the Pale were at first well inclined to the Government, and were only driven to the rebel side by the misconduct of the Lord Justices Parsons and Borlase, who, if any reliance can be placed on Carte's account, appear to have been two scoundrels desirous at heart of a good rebellion, with plenty of confiscations in its train. But the natural tendency of the course of events was to eliminate all moderation, and reduce the medley of parties to the two extremes,— that of the Ultramontanes on the one side, and that of the Cromwellians on the other. In the Councils of the Catholic Confederates the clergy, backed by the influence of foreign powers, soon obtained the lead; and a Papal legate arrived to preach war to extremity in the holy cause, and denounce all projects of accommodation. One Catholic bishop even took the command of the forces, and attacking Sir Charles Coote, who was strongly posted, lost his army and his life. Nothing less was contemplated by this party than to sever Ireland entirely from heretic England, and make it over to the dominion of some Catholic prince. Owen Roe O'Neil, to whom the military command on the side of the Confederates passed from his kinsman Sir Phelim, was a Continental soldier of distinction, and appears to have been a man of ability and character, capable of saving his country, if the Confederates could only have brought themselves to place the conduct of their enterprise fairly in his hands. But he was thwarted and overridden by the Pope's legate, and the impracticable fanatics who ruled the Council of Kilkenny. At the head of the Royalist party, Ormond, placed in a situation of worse than adversity, between the Scylla of Puritan rebellion on one hand and the Charybdis of Papist rebellion on the other, with an equivocal footing and a master on whom no dependence could be placed, displayed unwearied patience, steadiness, and self-control; and, whatever fondness for improving his own estate he may afterwards have shewn, fairly earned by his conduct in this desperate embroilment the name of a worthy, upright, and honourable gentleman. The King himself must be held by every candid judge of these events to have been entirely innocent of the original insurrection, except in so far as his perfidious refusal of the "graces" had added to the causes of discontent. Parsons and Borlase would gladly have presented the Parliament, whose sycophants they were, with evidence of his complicity; and they even endeavoured to extort such evidence by the infamous use of torture, the continued practice of which in Ireland, after it had been declared illegal and repudiated in England, is a proof of the backward state of the Irish Constitution. But these attempts to implicate Charles signally failed. Afterwards, when reduced to extremity, he tampered with the accursed thing, feebly, irresolutely, and mendaciously, as was his habit; and, as usual, to his own ruin.

The stronger race had, at the outset, been taken by

surprise, and received, before they were on their guard, a heavy and almost fatal blow. Their powers of resistance were further paralyzed, to a great extent, by the division of parties among themselves. Yet they held their ground against the Catholic Confederates, as the settlers of the Pale, when reduced to the verge of destruction, had held their ground against the ancient clans. The English Parliament, though its heart and the heart of the nation burned with fury at the tidings of the rebellion and massacre, was compelled to devote all its energies to the death-struggle with its nearer and more formidable foe. For aid to its friends in Ireland, it could only appeal to private adventurers, whom it paid by assignments of forfeited land, thus making the struggle internecine. At last the contest in England was brought to an end. Then, borne on the wings of victory and vengeance, Cromwell descended on the devoted land. It was not to be expected that the ecclesiastics who were at the head of the Irish Catholics, and who, as ecclesiastics, measured chances not by the forces at their own command but by those at the command of Heaven, should see the hopelessness of resistance to the terrible chief who now offered them, in a voice of doom, the choice between his sure clemency and his resistless sword. To the sword, accordingly, a brief and final appeal was made. The slaughter of the Catholic garrisons after the storm of Drogheda and Wexford is a dark blot on Cromwell's name. Unlike some of his admirers, he had the grace to excuse it on grounds of humanity, as being likely, by striking terror, in the end to save more blood. This excuse cannot be admitted. An example of atrocity, though it may cut short one war, tends to make all wars more atrocious. It is perhaps more to the purpose to observe that at the period of the Thirty Years' War the humane rules which now mitigate war had not been established. It was then a common thing to put to the sword the garrison and even the inhabitants of places which had been taken by storm. Protestant Europe had not forgotten the carnage of Magdeburgh. The provocation had been bitter. The demand for vengeance was loud. It is not too much to say that the English Puritans regarded the Irish Catholics, after O'Neil's massacre, with the rage of the Orangeman towards the Papist, added to the rage of the Englishman of Calcutta towards the Sepoy mutineer; and it may be fairly asserted that, under the circumstances of the case, and considering the state of opinion, Cromwell on the whole displayed the self-control and regard for humanity which became his greatness.

He was neither wicked nor weak enough to think of exterminating the Irish people. On the contrary, to the mass of them he at once extended a general amnesty, though he deprived the Catholics in Ireland, as well as in England, of the open exercise of a religion which all Protestants believed to be idolatrous, and knew by fearful experience to be persecuting. But he to a great extent dispossessed the old Irish proprietors, divided their lands among his victorious soldiery, and assigned them nominal compensations in Connaught. He also transported as slaves to the plantations many of those who had been engaged in the rebellion; and the low white population of the West Indies is probably descended in part from these sufferers, and from English Royalists who met with the same fate. This was hard measure, but it was far less hard than the measure which the Catholic House of Austria dealt at the same period to the Protestants of Bohemia and other provinces which were conquered in the Thirty Years' War.

The example of Ireland at the time of the English Revolution, and that of La Vendée at the time of the French Revolution, hold out a terrible warning to those who, without having made up their minds to face the worst, dabble in practices which may involve their country, as an insurgent province, in a mortal struggle with a great nation driven to take up arms as one man in defence of its own existence. In that extremity all the trammels which in ordinary times are imposed by the sensitiveness of wealth and civilization, or by old and cherished but feeble institutions, are fiercely swept aside. A terrible energy is put forth by the frame which seemed so languid and so unwilling to move. Men capable of commanding are propelled with volcanic force into the places of command; and when the moment of vengeance succeeds that of mortal fear, the voice of humanity is apt to lose its power.

Under the Protectorate the peace of complete submission reigned in Ireland, law was regularly administered, and the Protestant community at least presented a picture of prosperity such as the island had never before seen. But it is difficult to believe that the lot of the Irish Catholics can have been otherwise than hard under the domination of those fierce and fanatical children of the Old Covenant, who were dwelling in vineyards which they had not planted and houses which they had not built; who ranked the religion of the subdued race with idolatry, and who must have constantly read in the expressive faces of the people intense hatred mingled with cowering fear. To make Ireland like Yorkshire is said to have been the Protector's object; and this, as far as the nature of things permitted, his genius as a ruler achieved. But the nature of things rendered it impossible for him to do more than create a Yorkshire on the surface, while an Ireland still lay alien and vindictive below.

He governed the island partly as a dependency by the hand of that able and pure-minded son, who was worthy, if fate had permitted, to have inherited his glorious throne. Yet representatives of Ireland, as well as of Scotland, were called to his Parliaments; and there can be little doubt that had his life or the duration of his dynasty been prolonged, and had his designs taken full effect, the union of the two countries would have been completed. But in this, as in the rest of his policy, he was before his hour; and the few years of his reign, crowded with miracles of administrative genius, profound statesmanship, and high-souled diplomacy, gave only a transient glimpse of the great England that was to come.

The policy of the Restoration was in this as in other respects the opposite to that of Cromwell. Instead of completing the consolidation of the empire, it aimed at making both Scotland and Ireland entirely separate kingdoms; not out of regard for their independence, but that they might be cut off from the influence and protection of the still robust and formidable, though loyalist Parliament of England, and left more entirely under the arbitrary government of the Crown.

The few years of Cromwell's Protectorate had been sufficient to make the feelings of the landed proprietor stronger than those of the Republican and the sectary in the hearts of the Cromwellians of Ireland. They accepted the Restoration without much difficulty, but kept a firm grasp on their lands. In vain the Catholics and Royalists struggled for restitution; in vain they pleaded their innocence, their sufferings, their attachment to the Royal cause, and besieged all the avenues which led through purlieus of favouritism and corruption to the Restoration throne. The Ironsides were as wily and tenacious in diplomacy as they had been unconquerable in the field. The king himself, too, had blasted the hopes of the Catholics at the outset by declaring that he was for an English interest to be established in Ireland[g]. After an Iliad of controversy, bribery, and intrigue on the part of the claimants, and infinite wavering, temporizing, promising, and retracting on the part of the Government, the persevering energy of a compact and resolute interest, strong in possession, finally carried the day, and the Puritans kept the lands which had been meted to them by the sword. There is, in truth, scarcely an example in history of the overthrow of a political interest or settlement which has once fairly taken root in land. The Acts of Settlement and Explanation which closed the question of proprietorship, have been called the Great Charter of the

[g] Carte, bk. vi.

Irish Protestants. They were the Domesday Book of their disinherited opponents. The sentence had been given. Yet for many years after this time the title to a great part of the land in Ireland continued to be that of forcible and disputed possession; nor can the tenure of estates be said to have been perfectly secure for a quarter of a century after the final overthrow of the Romanizing House of Stuart. It is easy to imagine what effects general insecurity of title, and the presence of a body of adverse claimants, always brooding over their wrongs, and ready to rise for the recovery of their lost possessions, must have had on the political condition of the country and the progress of its civilization.

The good name of Ormond did not escape the aspersions of those bitter times. But he seems, as Lord Lieutenant, to have ruled the chaos of claims and counter-claims, passion and intrigue, with a wise and temperate hand, and to be chargeable solely with not having satisfied expectations which could have been satisfied only at the expense of a desperate civil war. He was one of those honourable old Cavaliers of the Constitutional type, whose leading statesman was Clarendon, and who soon gave way in the Councils of the Restoration to a school of politicians of a different stamp, the disciples of the Jesuits or of Hobbes, the slaves of France, the enemies of the Constitution, the unscrupulous partizans of arbitrary power. "I have no friends," said a suitor for court-favour to Ormond, "but God and your Grace." "Poor man," said Ormond, "you could not have two friends who have less interest at court."

It was during the struggle for the restitution of the confiscated lands, and with a view to influence the King in favour of the Catholic claims, that a party among the Catholics drew up the Loyal Remonstrance, in which they recognised the supremacy of the King in things temporal, any pretension of the See of Rome notwithstanding; denied the Pope's power of deposing princes; promised his Majesty their aid in defence of his person and authority against all foreign powers or authority whatsoever; and denounced as damnable the doctrine that heretic princes might be put to death by their subjects. This document met with little support among the priests; but a considerable number of the Catholic nobility and gentry were found willing to give it the sanction of their names.

The new conspirators against liberty, like Strafford and Laud before them, fixed on Ireland as a useful point of support for their designs, and Lord Berkeley appears to have been sent over by them as Lord Lieutenant to commence the game which in the ensuing reign was taken up and played out by Tyrconnell. They had not the scruples which Strafford and Laud, as sincere adherents of the Church of England, had felt in forming a compact alliance with the Catholic party; and it even appears that the "Remonstrants" were discouraged as too moderate for the new "Thorough." The unhappy but inevitable consequence was that the Irish Catholics were involved in the fury of the violent reaction which ensued, and that they furnished one of the most innocent victims to the sanguinary panic of the Popish Plot. It is needless to say that the murder of Archbishop Plunkett has left a deep stain on the ermine of English justice. But it must be remembered, in fairness to the English people, that though the Popish Plot denounced by Oates was a fiction, there was a Popish plot which was no fiction, but a reality of the most formidable kind. There was a Popish plot for the extirpation of Protestantism and liberty throughout Europe, of which the King of France was the powerful head, of which the Jesuits were the restless and unscrupulous agents, in which the King and the heir-presumptive to the crown were deeply engaged, and which all but overthrew the religion and liberties of England in the next reign.

It was not only in regard to her political affairs that Ireland suffered from the folly and selfishness of English statesmen during the reign of Charles II. A system of legislative restrictions upon Irish commerce, for the supposed protection of English interests, was now definitively adopted, which continued to poison the relations between the countries till, in the course of moral and intellectual progress, Adam Smith arose to set trade free. The jealousy of the English Protectionists appears to have been aroused by the sudden development of Irish commerce under Strafford, and again under Cromwell. A bill absolutely prohibiting the importation of Irish cattle into England was carried through Parliament with frantic violence. Those who ventured to oppose it were told that they must either have Irish estates or Irish understandings. The only question was whether the bounty of Providence in furnishing an abundant supply for a natural demand would be sufficiently stigmatized by calling it a "detriment," or whether it ought to be more strongly denounced as a "nuisance." The few men of sense ironically proposed that it should be made a felony or a *premunire;* and Clarendon drily suggested that it might as well be declared "adultery." Thus was England cut off, by the fatuous cupidity of her own legislators, from the only benefit which she could possibly have derived at that time from her connexion with Ireland; the estrangement of the two countries was deepened; and the hand which nature stretched out to heal the bleeding wound, was thrust back by the folly and perversity of man.

We have arrived at a period of Irish history which has been made familiar to all by a great writer. It would be as easy to sing of the siege of Troy after Homer, as to write about the siege of Londonderry after Macaulay. Immediately after the Reformation a great effort had been made by the Catholic powers and the Papacy, under the leadership of Spain, to put down Protestantism, and the political liberty which Protestantism brought in its train. This effort was defeated mainly by the combined efforts of Holland and England. It was renewed on a different scene by the House of Austria in the Thirty Years' War, and there again defeated by Gustavus Adolphus; while a sympathetic movement in favour of absolutism, commenced in England by Charles I. and his councillors, was defeated by the Puritans and Cromwell. Absolutism and Catholicism again found a powerful champion in Louis XIV., who acted on England through his subsidized satraps, the later Stuarts; and Ireland was once more drawn into the vortex of the struggle which ensued. James II., following the lead of the Cabal and Strafford, attempted to make of Ireland a useful instrument for his designs against the religion and constitution of the less tractable country. The Irish people, it has been justly observed, in entering on the civil war, were moved, not by attachment to the House of Stuart or to its political principles, but, like the Highland clans, by local motives of their own. The leader round whom they rallied was in fact not James II. but Tyrconnell. In that descendant of the degenerate English of the Pale appeared upon the scene for the last time the faint image of an old Irish chief. The Catholic clergy could not fail to enter with heart and soul into a cause which was that of their religion. But probably the mass of James's party, though they were fighting for the Catholic religion, were fighting less for the Catholic religion, than for that old and terrible subject of Irish civil wars, the land. The sweeping Acts of confiscation and proscription passed by the Irish Parliament of James, were in effect a violent and vindictive reversal of the Acts of Settlement and Explanation, by which the lands of the Catholics had been finally made over to the Cromwellians.

The country being in a state of the most fearful anarchy and ferment, the lives of Protestants were everywhere in danger, and many outrages were committed; but it does not appear that the Catholic leaders, while they dispossessed and proscribed the intrusive proprietors, and held over their heads the menace of death, intended actually to shed their blood. The war, however, was waged on both sides with the ferocity for which civil wars are notorious, the Catholics on one side driving a helpless population to die under the walls of Londonderry, the Enniskilleners on the other cutting down their defeated enemies without mercy; and a harvest of hate and vengeance was laid up sufficient to account for much that would otherwise seem too bad for human nature during some generations to come.

In England, Cromwell may be said to have risen again, after the reactionary interval of the Restoration, in the person of William III., though in a more Constitutional form. In Ireland, in the same manner, William was a milder Cromwell. His calm and lofty mind, raised above fanaticism by converse with great affairs, expanded by intercourse with the rulers and diplomatists of various nations, and rendered liberal by the habit of acting in alliance with men of different creeds, disposed him to statesmanlike toleration, and rendered him unwilling to be the tool of any narrow and persecuting faction. In accepting the oath tendered to him by the Scotch Parliament as the condition of their adhesion, he expressly protested that he would not be a persecutor; and it was in the spirit of that protest that he and the best representatives of his policy shewed themselves inclined to act towards the defeated party in Ireland. Those who invoke the name of William of Orange at the orgies of tyrannical faction, do that name a grievous wrong. A constitutional king, with confined and precarious powers, on a throne beset by factions, and threatened by a Pretender, he could of course do little to stem the torrent of fanaticism and vengeance; but what he could do, he did; and he braved odium by liberal grants of pardons and restorations of forfeited lands [h]. In truth, the glorious blood of Orange could scarcely have run in a low persecutor's veins.

At the conclusion of each of the great civil wars in Ireland, in the time of the Tudors, in that of Charles I., and in that of James II., large numbers of Irish soldiers took foreign service. The civil war of James II. gave rise to the famous Irish brigade in the service of France. The Irish have given generals and marshals to the armies of France, Spain, Austria, Russia, and Sardinia; they have produced magnates of the Empire and grandees of Spain. They renewed the war against England under the banners of her enemies. Their valour was arrayed against her at Ramillies, Almanza, and Laufeldt. She encountered it in the service of Spain at Gibraltar; she encountered it under Lally at Pondicherry; and it turned the day against the iron steadfastness of her infantry at Fontenoy. The Irish blood has given a ruler to Spain in the person of O'Donnell; it has given a hero, and it may give a ruler, to France in the person of McMahon. On the banners of these exiles sat much glory and some shame. Italians were the plotting head, but Irishmen were the murderous hand of the conspiracy which assassinated Wallenstein.

We are moved with pity and indignation when we turn to the records of these mournful emigrations, and

[h] See O'Connor on Irish Catholics, p. 157.

see the lists of brave Irish youth who were driven forth to shed their blood in foreign fields. But these were not the only men whom the evil spirit of those persecuting times had turned into soldiers and exiles. A French Huguenot regiment in the service of King William was engaged in the battle of the Boyne; and it was cheered on to the charge by its commander with the cry "Gentlemen, your persecutors are before you." And if Irish names, the monuments of undeserved misfortunes, are common in the Catholic countries of the Continent, French names, the monuments of misfortunes equally undeserved, are not rare in Ireland.

With the conclusion of the war between William and James commences, properly speaking, the reign of Protestant Ascendancy, and of the Persecuting Code. In the last struggle the Protestant and Catholic interests respectively had been completely identified with the bodies of rival claimants to the land; and the persecution of the Catholics was a policy which served equally the purposes of religious bigotry and that of territorial fear.

Hitherto the legal disabilities and the grievances under which the Irish Catholics laboured had been comparatively trifling; and, in particular, they had enjoyed full political rights, possessing the electoral franchise, and being admissible to both Houses of Parliament[1]. It was the danger into which they had brought

---

[1] Macaulay (vol. ii. p. 127) thus contrasts the condition of the Irish with that of the English Catholics in the reign of James II. "The grievances under which the members of his (James's) Church laboured in Ireland, differed widely from those which he was attempting to remove in England and Scotland. The Irish Statute-book, afterwards polluted by intolerance as barbarous as that of the dark ages, then con-

the empire, and the proscription lists which they had drawn up under James II., that drew upon them the penal code. Some of the articles of that code, such as the one prohibiting the employment of Roman Catholics as gamekeepers, are so extravagantly absurd, as to shew that it was the work not so much of a cold-blooded policy as of frantic rage and fear. Land has been the great source of contention and misery in Ireland throughout her history. The question of the monastery lands affected the conduct of a great party in England, and the course of English politics, perhaps as far down as the Revolution of 1688, and the Acts of Settlement and Explanation had at least as great an influence on the action of parties and the course of affairs in the other island.

It has been observed that the articles of the Persecuting Code which were directed against the religion of the Catholics were less actively enforced than those which were directed against their social and territorial influence; and M. Gustave de Beaumont, in a work upon

tained scarce a single enactment, and not a single stringent enactment imposing any penalty on Papists as such. On one side of St. George's Channel every priest who received a neophyte into the bosom of the Church of Rome was liable to be hanged, drawn, and quartered. On the other side he incurred no such danger. A Jesuit who landed at Dover took his life in his hand: but he walked the streets of Dublin in security. Here no man could hold office, or earn his livelihood as a barrister or a schoolmaster, without previously taking the oath of supremacy; but in Ireland a public functionary was not held to be under the necessity of taking that oath unless it were formally tendered to him. It therefore did not exclude from employment any one whom the government wished to promote. The sacramental test and the declaration against transubstantiation were unknown: nor was either House of Parliament closed against any religious sect.

Irish history, written on the charitable theory that England has systematically sought to exterminate the Irish people, allows in effect that the persecution was intermittent, and that the sharpest moments were those when the dominant party was threatened by the attempts of the Pretender or the arms of the Catholic powers. In truth it was one of the last consequences of a great general cause which had filled Christendom for two centuries with fratricidal war, and the evil influence of which was in all countries but just beginning to abate.

The code, in truth, stands in need of all the palliations which the largest and calmest view of history can afford; and when all those palliations have been exhausted, its memory will still remain a reproach to human nature, and a terrible monument of the vileness into which nations may be led when their religion has been turned into hatred, and they have been taught to believe that the indulgence of the most malignant passions of man is an acceptable offering to God. For it was a code of degradation and proscription, not only religious and political, but social. It denied to the persecuted sect the power of educating their children at home, and at the same time, with an almost maniacal cruelty, it prohibited them from seeking education abroad. It disabled them from acquiring freehold property. It subjected their estates to an exceptional rule of succession, a reproduction, in fact, of that very custom of gavelkind which had been abolished as barbarous, with a view to break them into fragments, and thus destroy the territorial power of the Catholic proprietors. It excluded them from the liberal and influential professions. It took from them the guardianship of their own children. It endeavoured to set child against parent, and parent against child, by the truly diabolical enactment that the son of a Papist, on turning Protestant, should dispossess his father of the fee simple of his estate; the father's estate, even in that which he had himself acquired, being reduced to a lifeinterest, while the reversion vested absolutely in the son, as a reward for his conversion to the true religion. It would not be difficult to point to persecuting laws more sanguinary than these. Spain, France, and Austria, will at once supply signal examples. But it would be difficult to point to any more insulting to the best feelings of man, or more degrading to religion.

As if to prevent the possibility of reconciliation between the two creeds and races, intermarriages between Catholics and Protestants, possessing any estate in Ireland, were forbidden. It seems, indeed, as though the persecutors had intended almost to exclude their victims from the pale of human society. For in the case of alleged offences against certain of the penal laws, the first principles of criminal justice were deliberately and ostentatiously set aside, by removing the burden of proof from the accuser and casting it on the accused.

In the case of the Catholic priesthood, the persecution, legally at least, did not stop short of blood. Regular priests, bishops, and other ecclesiastics claiming jurisdiction, and all who should come into the kingdom from foreign parts, were banished on pain of transportation, in case of their neglecting to comply, and of the punishment of high treason in case of their returning from banishment. To prevent evasion priests were required to be registered; they were forbidden to leave their own parishes; and rewards were held out to informers who should detect the violations of these statutes, to be levied on the popish inhabitants of the country. Practically speaking, though informers drove their infamous trade, blood was not shed. Had blood been shed, it is reasonable as well as charitable to believe that the code, instead of being gradually abolished by a hard and protracted struggle, would at once have been torn in pieces by the indignation of the English people. It endured longer than the persecuting laws of the Catholic monarchies, partly because it was less atrocious. Hallam has remarked on the system that "to have exterminated the Catholics by the sword, or expelled them, like the Moriscoes of Spain, would have been a little more repugnant to justice and humanity, but incomparably more politic." The policy which was actually pursued was such as the opinion of the age still rendered practicable. But the opinion even of that age would have protested against extermination. Yet the extermination of heretics had only just ceased to be possible. Men must have been still living, when the worst of the penal laws were enacted, who remembered among the earliest events of their childhood, the atrocities committed by the Piedmontese Catholics on the Protestants of Savoy. The revocation of the Edict of Nantes, the Dragonnades, the expulsion of the French Protestants, were yet fresh in the minds of men. Not only so, but an Irish ecclesiastic who had been in

Spain might, when beset by informers, and treated as a Pariah by the professors of the dominant creed, still have reason to feel that his lot was more tolerable than the lot of the heretics, who were even then exposed to the fangs of the Inquisition, and in danger of being dragged by it to the stake. The last persecuting Act against Irish and English Catholics had been passed, and a reaction of feeling towards toleration had commenced, before *Autos da Fè* had ceased to be celebrated with public pomp and recorded with pious satisfaction.

That persecution was the vice of an age and not only of a particular religion, that it disgraced Protestantism as well as Catholicism, is true. But no one who reads the religious history of Europe with an open mind can fail to perceive that the persecutions carried on by Protestants were far less bloody and less extensive than those carried on by Catholics; that they were more frequently excusable as acts of retaliation; that they arose more from political alarm and less from the spirit of the religion; and that the temper of their authors yielded more rapidly to the advancing influence of humanity and civilization.

In the negotiations for the treaty of Ryswick, efforts were made by the Catholic powers to obtain a measure of indulgence for the Irish Catholics; but those efforts were frustrated by the obstinate refusal of Louis XIV. to consent, on his part, to any relaxations in favour of the Huguenots. On the other hand, the Penal Code paralyzed the endeavours of the English Government when it attempted to obtain from the Emperor of Germany indulgences for the Protestants of his empire. Those who wish to give a calm and just view of Irish history, cannot present this connexion of events too often or too clearly.

The Protestant Bishop Mant, in his history of the Irish Church[j], says of some of the most cruel of the Penal Laws, that they were enactments "of which some may condemn the severity, and others may lament the necessity." Of others, including the abominable law "for restraining from foreign education," he observes[k], that "they were not penal statutes enacted against the Romanists, but they were statutes of precaution for the security of the National Church and the peace and prosperity of the kingdom." He thinks the character of Archbishop Marsh, the avowed framer of the bill for preventing Protestants from intermarrying with Papists, a sufficient voucher for the prudence and justice of that bill. He cites with perfect satisfaction the preamble of the statute preventing Papists from being solicitors, which states as a reason for that iniquity that "Papist solicitors have been and still are, the common disturbers of the peace and tranquillity of his Majesty's subjects in general." The statute prohibiting the Catholic people from observing the holydays of their Church, was, in the opinion of the same respectable prelate, "a great indulgence and benefit to the large body of the Popish population, by exempting them, many days in the year, from the obligation to unprofitable inaction, and the temptation to spend a very large portion of their time in idleness, drunkenness, and vice; and enabling and encouraging them to

[j] Vol. ii. p. 136.   [k] p. 77.

employ it in honest and profitable industry." Persecution, like slavery, is doubly cursed: it depraves the intellect and heart of the oppressor as much as it destroys the moral dignity and the happiness of the oppressed.

The Established Church of Ireland could only become national, in any but an ironical sense, by winning over to its communion the bulk of the nation. And its one chance of winning them over was by recognising the common Christianity of Protestants and Catholics, and charitably embracing whatever was good in the Catholic system. But how could the Church of the dominant minority do this without at the same time acknowledging that Ascendancy and the system of intolerance were outrages on reason, justice, and religion? Its clergy were compelled, on the contrary, to exaggerate the falsehood and the evil of Roman Catholicism, in order to justify their own position as ministers of a Christian Church placed on the neck of another Christian Church by a sheer exertion of political power. This is a source of bitterness, religious and social, which, while the two Churches remain in their present position, can scarcely ever cease to flow.

Such a Protestant as Berkeley indeed could address to the Roman Catholic Priesthood of Ireland a pastoral letter on their duty to their flocks, appealing, in language worthy of his admirable character, to their common Christianity. Yet in this appeal he could not avoid unconsciously betraying the unsoundness of his ecclesiastical position. If the Roman Catholic clergy were his "countrymen, his fellow subjects, and believers in the same Christ" in the full sense of those terms, why should his Church be the object of State favour and theirs of State persecution? If they were really as capable as his exhortations imply of making their people all that the Government would desire the people to be, why should not the Government, instead of treating them as a class of criminals, summon them to discharge and pay them for discharging the duties which they, who alone possessed the confidence and affection of the people, were manifestly the best fitted to perform? "Be not startled, reverend Sirs, to find yourselves addressed by one of a different communion. We are, indeed, (to our shame be it spoken,) more inclined to hate for those articles wherein we differ, than to love one another for those wherein we agree. But if we cannot extinguish, let us at least suspend our animosities, and, forgetting our religious feuds, consider ourselves in the amiable light of countrymen and neighbours. Let us for once turn our eyes on those things in which we have one common interest. Why should disputes about faith interrupt the duties of civil life? or the different roads we take to heaven prevent our taking the same steps on earth? Do we not inhabit the same spot of ground, breathe the same air, and live under the same government? Why then should we not conspire in one and the same design, to promote the common good of our country?" When such language as this is held by a Prelate of a dominant establishment protected by cruel penal laws, are we to take it as serious or as ironical? The letter concludes with the expression of a sincere wish that there was no other contest between the writer's Church and the Roman Catholics, but *who should most completely practise the precepts of Him by whose name they were called, and whose disciples they all professed to be.* Did Berkeley remember that one of those precepts was to do to others as you would be done by? And had he considered whether he and his Church were doing by the Catholics as they would the Catholics should do by them? Had he, in short, at all examined the foundations of the extraordinary institution to which he belonged? Perhaps he had, for he was glad to turn from the Church of Ireland and its concerns to a more hopeful mission in a distant sphere.

That age is past. But it is still useful to remember that not a century has elapsed since a large party in a civilized and Christian country thought to maintain true religion by connecting it with injustice, and to secure to the State the allegiance of a mass of its subjects by giving them the most overwhelming reasons for disaffection.

The most detestable of the Penal Laws, morally speaking, were those which bribed conversion by enabling convert children to dispossess their parents; but the worst were those which denied to the mass of the people and to their clergy the liberty of education. "To render men patient," said Burke, "under deprivation of all the rights of human nature, everything which could give them a knowledge or feeling of those rights was rationally forbidden. To render humanity fit to be insulted, it was fit that it should be degraded." The love of the Irish for knowledge is great. It broke forth, as we have seen, with singular strength in the earliest period of their history; it has broken forth again with the same strength now that the means of education are once more afforded to them. It was not entirely quenched even by the Penal Laws, or by the social misery which prevailed during the same period. Hedge-schools were set up, when to open a regular school was forbidden; and the country presented the singular spectacle of a people, feebly but earnestly struggling to attain knowledge and intelligence, while ignorance and brutality were imposed upon them by the law.

Even those philosophers who think that religion is a thing of the past, and that philosophy and science are to govern the future, allow that during the past, religious influence has been a principal element of civilization. The natural character of the Irish could not fail to be degraded through the degradation of their religion. It was impossible that a clergy denied the means of education should raise the intelligence of their people. It was almost impossible that a clergy, themselves the victims of the most outrageous oppression, should diffuse around them love of the Government and the feelings of a good citizen. It is an honour to the Catholic priesthood that they should have kept the hearts of the people, as they appear on the whole to have kept them, warm, affectionate, and open to kindly influences; and that by their example, as well as by their preaching, they should have almost extirpated vices to which, as we have seen, the native character of the Irish was prone, and to which the French are still addicted.

We have already, in considering the origin of the

Established Church of Ireland, noticed the fatal impediments which, from the nature of the case, beset its action and rendered it inherently incapable of supplying to the people the place of a national Church. Even its most obvious work, that of preaching to the natives in the native tongue, and circulating among them an Irish version of the Scriptures, though it was not forgotten, and though it was urged on at times with some vigour by Bedell and other conscientious men, was on the whole very feebly performed. James II. issued a mandate nominating a Papist to the Professorship of the Irish language in Trinity College. It turned out that no such Professorship existed. The king's breach of the law was without excuse, but he might be excused for his misapprehension. The duty of founding schools for the education of the Irish in the same manner, though not wholly neglected, was feebly prosecuted. Those which were founded became infected with the prevailing spirit of torpor and corruption; and being inevitably tainted with proselytism, they were from the outset objects of suspicion to the people.

Even as a school of theology, the Established Church of Ireland could not fail to be injuriously affected by the circumstances in which it was placed. As it was planted like a hostile garrison in the dominions of Roman Catholicism, and had its very being in antagonism to that religion, its Protestantism was almost necessarily polemical and extreme. This influence has formed one side of its theological character. Another side was formed by the strong secular influences to which Irish Churchmen were subjected, and which are apt to produce in all Churchmen whom they affect, a certain hardness and coarseness of mind, and a want of high spiritual aspirations. The high spiritualism of Berkeley appears to have found little favour with the learned among his brother prelates. It was far less congenial to the character of a dominant and political Church, than the hard and forbidding view of the Divine Character and Government contained in such a work as Archbishop King's treatise on the "Origin of Evil." No man or Church can speculate worthily on spiritual subjects without a mind perfectly clear, free, and turned without reserve or misgiving towards the source of truth. An equivocal position is fatal to thought as well as to action. Church History, written by the members of a Church so situated as the Church of Ireland, could not fail to be of a narrow character. No doubt there have been Irish divines free from these tendencies. Tendencies may be very strong, but they are not fate.

It is to be said in further excuse of the long inefficiency of the Established Church, that it was left by the Tudors in the most miserable state of dilapidation. The account given by Spenser of its state is deplorable. In the time of Charles I. Bramhall wrote to Laud, "It is hard to say whether the churches be more ruinous and sordid, or the people irreverent, even in Dublin, the metropolis of this kingdom, and seat of justice." A parochial church had been converted into the Lord Deputy's stable, a second into a nobleman's dwelling-house, the choir of a third into a tennis-court, the vicar acting as the keeper. The vaults under Christ's Church had been made into tippling-rooms for beer, wine, and tobacco. After the time of which Bramhall speaks came the ravages of the Civil Wars; and the fabrics and revenues of the Church were scarcely restored to a tolerable state before the middle of the eighteenth century, by which time much had been done by the exertions of such men as Boulter, who, if they were rather statesmen than Churchmen, were men of business, and shewed vigour in improving the pecuniary interests and reforming the order and organization of their Church. The laity of the dominant faction, while they regarded the Establishment as a necessary political instrument, treated it, as was natural, with little respect or justice. They were as ready to plunder it as they were to oppress its antagonist in its name.

The Catholics were completely prostrated by the persecution. They did not lift their heads when the banner of the Stuarts was raised again, either in 1715, or in 1745. The only political parties in Ireland were two factions which gradually developed themselves in the interior of the privileged caste, one calling itself the English, the other the Irish interest. These two factions were equally selfish, equally worthless, and equally alien to the mass of the Irish people. The faction of the English interest aimed at keeping Ireland in the state of a dependency, and appropriating the offices and the Church preferment to Englishmen. The faction of the Irish interest wished to be an independent oligarchy, sharing the power of tyranny and the prizes of domination among themselves. The faction of the Irish interest was instinctively led to struggle against the restrictions on Irish trade; but in other respects it is probable that one who cared for the mass of the Irish people would have sympathized rather with the faction of the English interest, as representing in some degree at least an imperial policy, and imperial objects, whereas the policy and objects of the Irish interest were merely those of a tyrannical caste. Swift espoused the side of the Irish interest; but he probably did so principally to indulge a restless and embittered spirit, which craved for agitation, and was eager to make war on any pretext, and under any banner, against a Hanoverian administration. He who has been dignified with the name of an Irish patriot, and whose shade was invoked by Grattan at the inauguration of Irish independence, was promoted to an Irish Deanery by English interest for services rendered to an English party; and he cynically disclaimed all personal connexion with the "vile country," which would fain place him in its Pantheon. The farcical panic about Wood's halfpence, to which the author of the Drapier's Letters condescended to pander, is a fair measure of the reasonableness and dignity of Irish politics at that time. Molyneux, the friend and disciple of Locke, was a more respectable advocate of the views of the same party: but he much mistook the sentiments of his master if he thought that an uncontrolled oligarchy would have satisfied the great teacher of civil and religious freedom. The Lord Lieutenancy being regarded as half a sinecure, and its holder being frequently resident in England, the English interest was managed to a great extent through ecclesiastics, who thus resumed the equivocal functions which had been exercised by their order during the middle ages. The most remarkable of these episcopal politicians was Primate Boulter, whose correspondence gives us a singular picture of a system of political management, of which patronage was the mainspring, as the retention of patronage was its principal aim. Boulter's successor, Primate Stone, called, from the handsomeness of his person only, "the beauty of holiness," condescended, unless he is much maligned, to secure the support of the young Irish aristocracy by expedients compared with which the most profligate use of patronage was pure. His palace is said to have rivalled those of the Prince Bishops of Germany in offering every possible provision for the tastes of the most voluptuous guests. Irish government during the eighteenth century is, in fact, one of the foulest places of history; and it is enough to know its character and to pass it by.

The energy of the Protestant part of the community caused it to advance in commercial prosperity, notwithstanding the trammels which the Protectionist Parliaments of England continued to impose. But the mass of the people were socially and economically in a state the most deplorable perhaps which history records as having existed in any civilized nation. If a parallel is to be found it must be in some of the French provinces, at the calamitous close of the reign of Louis XIV., or on the eve of the Revolution.

The Cromwellian landowners soon lost their religious character, while they retained all the hardness of the fanatic, and the feelings of Puritan conquerors towards a conquered Catholic people. "I have eaten with them," said one, "drunk with them, played with them, fought with them; but I never prayed with them." Their descendants became probably the very worst upper class with which a country was ever afflicted. The habits of the Irish gentry grew beyond measure brutal and reckless, and the coarseness of their debaucheries would have disgusted the crew of Comus[1]. Their drunkenness, their blasphemy, their ferocious duelling, left the squires of England far behind. If there was a grotesque side to their vices which mingles laughter with our reprobation, this did not render their influence less pestilent to the community of which the malice of destiny had made them the social chiefs. Fortunately their recklessness was sure, in the end, to work, to a certain extent, its own cure; and in the background of their swinish and uproarious drinking bouts, the Encumbered Estates Act rises to our view.

Over the Roman Catholic poor on their estates, these "vermin of the kingdom," as Arthur Young, in his "Tour in Ireland," calls them, exercised a tyranny compared with which the arbitrary rule of the old chiefs over their clans was probably a parental authority used with beneficence, and justly repaid by gratitude and affection. The clansman was not, like the Roman Catholic peasant, "disarmed;" he did not "speak a language which was despised, and profess a religion which was abhorred." "A landlord in Ireland," says Arthur Young, in a passage which has been frequently

[1] See especially the opening chapters of Barrington's Sketches.

quoted, "can scarcely invent an order which a servant, labourer or cottar, dares to refuse to execute. Nothing satisfies him but unlimited submission. Disrespect, or anything tending towards sauciness, he may punish with his cane or his horsewhip with the most perfect security. A poor man would have his bones broken if he offered to lift his hand in his own defence. Knocking down is spoken of in the country in a manner that makes an Englishman stare. Landlords of consequence have assured me that many of their cottars would think themselves honoured by having their wives and daughters sent for to the bed of their master, a mark of slavery which proves the oppression under which such people must live. Nay, I have heard anecdotes of the lives of people being made free with, without any apprehension of the justice of a jury. But let it not be imagined that this is common; formerly it happened every day, but law gains ground. It must strike the most careless traveller, to see whole strings of cars whipt into a ditch by a gentleman's footman, to make way for his carriage; if they are overturned or broken in pieces, no matter, it is taken in patience: were they to complain they would perhaps be horsewhipped. The execution of the laws lies very much in the hands of the justices of the peace, many of whom are drawn from the most illiberal class in the kingdom. If a poor man lodges his complaint against a gentleman, or any animal that chooses to call itself a gentleman, and the justice issues out a summons for his appearance, it is a fixed affront, and he will infallibly be *called out*. Where *manners* are in conspiracy against *law*, to whom are the oppressed people to have recourse? It is a fact, that a poor man, having a contest with a gentleman, must—but I am talking nonsense; they know their situation too well to think of it; they can have no defence but by means of protection from one gentleman against another, who probably protects his vassal as he would the sheep he intends to eat."

The author of "An Inquiry into the Causes of Popular Discontents in Ireland[m]," states that "it has not been unusual in Ireland for great landed proprietors to have regular prisons in their houses, for the summary punishment of the lower orders." Not a century has passed since these ruffians and tyrants filled, in Ireland, the seat of justice. How many centuries of a widely different training have the English people gone through in order to acquire their boasted love of law!

Nothing is so rapacious as profusion; no landlord is so extortionate as one who is sensual and reckless. The Irish landlords, while they squandered their substance in the indulgence of insane pride as well as of gross licentiousness, were grinding their poor tenants to the dust. By all who had occasion to speak of the misery of the people, from Swift down to Lord Charlemont, the cry was raised against the extortions of the landlord and of his middlemen. The first and original causes of Whiteboyism are stated by Lord Charlemont to have been "exorbitant rents, low wages, want of employment in a country destitute of manufactures, where desolation and famine were the effects of fertility; where the rich gifts of a bountiful mother were de-

---

[m] Quoted by Sir G. C. Lewis, "On Irish Disturbancy," p. 53.

structive to her children, and served only to tantalize them; where oxen supplied the place of men, and by leaving little room for cultivation, while they enriched their pampered owners, starved the miserable remnant of thinly scattered inhabitants: farms of enormous extent, let by their rapacious and indolent proprietors to monopolizing land-jobbers, by whom small portions of them were again let and relet to intermediate oppressors, and by them subdivided for five times their value, among the wretched starvers upon potatoes and water: taxes yearly increasing, and tithes which the Catholic, without any possible benefit, unwillingly pays in addition to his priest-money: misery, oppression, and famine." The Tory Fitzgibbon, afterwards Lord Clare, would not have been disposed to exaggerate the miseries of a system of which he was a leading supporter: yet he said in a debate on tithes,—"The lower orders of the people in Munster are in a state of depression and abject poverty, sloth, dirt, and misery not to be equalled in any other part of the world. But this cannot be ascribed to the clergy,—far from it,—it is owing in the first place to their own indolence, and in the next to a set of men called middlemen; a set of gentry who, having no inheritance, no education, or other means of life, than by getting between the inheritor and the cultivator of the soil, grind the poor people to powder."

Lord Clare is not alone in placing the "indolence" of the people first among the causes of their distress. But had he himself been denied the benefit of education, shut out from all hope of improving his condition, and racked by a middleman, he would perhaps not have possessed the buoyancy and energy of mind, or have been capable of the vigorous exertions, which raised him so high in the profession of the law.

Absenteeism, as well as middlemen, had become a cause of bitter complaints in the time of Swift, who includes in the general picture of misery "the old seats of the nobility and gentry all in ruins, and no new ones in their stead." It was natural that the gentry should avoid the sight of so much wretchedness; it was natural that their vain and frivolous natures should be drawn to the pleasures of Dublin or London; and they had neither sufficiently fine feelings nor a sufficient intellectual interest in social objects and improvements to keep them in the path of social duty. We have had occasion to observe in reference to the absenteeism of early Irish history that the money drawn away by absentees, though it is the common ground of complaint, is not the greatest evil of absenteeism. Wherever that money is spent it will be spent mainly in the employment of unproductive labour, and will consequently do little to increase the wealth of a country. The greatest evils of absenteeism are, first, that it withdraws from the community its upper class, who are the natural channels of civilizing influences to the classes below them; and secondly, that it cuts off all personal relations between the individual landlord and his tenant, closes up the compassion of the landlord, and exposes the tenant to a pressure as unfeeling and relentless as that of a hand of iron. It also has necessarily a general, though not an invariable tendency to prevent the improvement of the land.

No doubt there were kind landlords in Ireland, even in her worst days; and to these the hearts of the peasantry seem to have turned with all the affectionate loyalty which they had once rendered to their ancient chiefs. Sir Jonah Barrington has given us, at the commencement of his "Sketches of his own Times," an account, exaggerated, no doubt, but partly credible, of what he justly calls the "somewhat feudal" life of a good Irish squire surrounded by his retainers. It is the "spend me and defend me" of Spenser's time over again. "At the Great House all disputes amongst the tenants were then settled, quarrels reconciled, old debts arbitrated; a kind landlord reigned despotic in the ardent affections of the tenantry, their pride and pleasure being to obey and support him. But there existed a happy reciprocity of interests. The landlord of that period protected his tenant by his influence, any wanton injury to the tenant being considered as an insult to the lord; and if either of the landlord's sons were grown up, no time was lost by him in demanding satisfaction from any gentleman for maltreating even his father's blacksmith." Sir Jonah adds, that "no gentleman of this degree ever distrained a tenant for rent." In illustration of this happy state of feeling he tells two family anecdotes, one of his father's tenants having met together after their own hard day's work to reap a field of their landlord's corn which was over-ripe, and having, with characteristic delicacy, concealed from their landlord the names of those who had rendered him the service; the other (which must rest on his authority alone) of a lady

of the family who wished in the hearing of her faithful
domestics for the ears of an impudent squireen, and was
soon afterwards presented with a box, on opening
which, she started to find that her wish had been
affectionately fulfilled [n].

There was but one drawback, according to Sir Jonah's
account, to this social felicity. It was the tithe-proctor,
of whom there prevailed "the greatest abhorrence,
coupled with no great predilection for the clergy who
employed them." When tithes were in question, the
Irish landlord was a Whiteboy. The clergy claimed
the tithe of agistment, that is, of pasturage for dry
and barren cattle. The law decided in favour of their
claim; but the landlords who ruled the Irish House of
Commons passed a resolution, "that all legal ways and
means ought to be made use of, to oppose all attempts
that shall hereafter be framed to carry demands of tithe
agistment into execution, until a proper remedy can be
provided by the legislature." Associations were formed
in the different counties by the landlords assembled at
the assizes; in each county a common purse was made
up for supporting any lawsuit against the clergy; "who
were moreover," says Bishop Mant [o], "threatened with
opposition and distress in the maintenance of their
other rights, if they ventured to sue for agistment;
and were treated with a degree of hostility and male-
volence which, by moderate and sensible men, was

---

[n] It is as well to mention that Sir Jonah Barrington held no less
a position than that of Judge of the High Court of Admiralty in
Ireland.

[o] History of the Irish Church, vol. ii. p. 556.

thought equal to any signs of ill-will ever remembered to have been manifested against the Popish priests in the most dangerous times." The landlords, according to Archbishop Boulter, "had let their lands so high, that, without robbing the clergy of their just dues, they were satisfied their rents could hardly be paid." The Whiteboy was equally satisfied that without a similar resistance to legal claims, he and his family could not live. It was not in his power to dignify his associations by forming them at the assizes; nor were a common purse and legal chicanery placed by fortune at his command.

Under such masters, and after a course of events so fatal to order, industry, and everything appertaining to the moral and physical welfare of a nation, the condition of the people could not fail to be wretched. In the year 1729, Swift wrote, in the capital of the kingdom,—"It is a melancholy object to those who walk through this great town, or travel in the country, when they see the streets, the roads and cabin-doors crowded with beggars of the female sex, followed by three, four, or six children, all in rags, and importuning every passenger for an alms. These mothers, instead of being able to work for their honest livelihood, are forced to employ all their time in strolling to beg sustenance for their helpless infants; who, as they grow up, either turn thieves for want of work, or leave their dear native country to fight for the pretender in Spain, or sell themselves to the Barbadoes[p]." With ghastly pleasantry, he suggested that it would be a good thing if

[p] "A Modest Proposal."

Ireland had the privilege of selling her surplus population for slaves [q]; and with still more ghastly pleasantry he put forth a "Modest Proposal," that a certain number of the useless infants should be consigned to the butcher [r]. He had been assured by "a very skilful computer," that "above one-half of the souls in the kingdom supported themselves by begging and thieving." The computation was no doubt extravagant, but Swift would not have credited it if the mass of compulsory idleness and destitution before his eyes had not been very great.

Yet at this time the population of Ireland was by Swift's reckoning only a million and a-half. Down to the end of the preceding century the increase of population had been effectually checked by decimating wars. The civil war in the time of Charles I. alone was reckoned to have swept off nearly seven hundred thousand souls. The long tranquillity of the eighteenth century removed this terrible restraint; and an increase of population then set in, which entailed sufferings worse in themselves, and far worse in their moral consequences, than the sharp stroke of war. This miserable race of serfs multiplied in their recklessness and despair till the population of the island had risen from a million and a half to eight millions: at that point the Great Famine of 1846 arrived to close one of the most horrible episodes in the annals of mankind. During this period the increase in the productive powers of the land, owing to the recklessness and bankruptcy of the landlords, had been slow; and the increase of trade and manu-

[q] "Maxims Controlled in Ireland."   [r] "Modest Proposal."

factures among the Protestants of the north might almost as well, so far as the mass of the peasantry were concerned, have been going on in a distant nation.

All moral restraints on the increase of population were removed by the compulsory ignorance into which Protestant Ascendancy and the Penal Laws had plunged the Catholic peasantry, and by the abject wretchedness of their lot. The very names of providence and frugality would have been a mockery if uttered in their ears. No idea of comfort or cleanliness could find place in their minds. No wonder that they wallowed, swine-like, among their swine. The finest gentleman in England, placed in their condition, would have been as they were. The economical virtues of man are dependent on circumstances: to produce them in him, or to wean him from the opposite vices, you must place him in favourable circumstances: preaching and penalties are alike vain.

The natural question is, how could the people manage to support life? The answer to that question is, that not a few of them managed to support life by mixing potatoes with seaweed, and by taking but one meal of this wretched food a-day[s]. Had they even been previously imbued with the most confirmed habits of industry, such diet must have produced physical inability to work.

In the time of Elizabeth, Raleigh, ever active and inventive, had introduced the potato on his Irish 'plan-

---

[s] See the extracts from Evidence taken before a Committee of the House of Commons, on the State of the Poor in Ireland, given by Sir G. C. Lewis, "On Irish Disturbances," p. 91.

tation.' The gift, than which the Archfiend could scarcely have offered anything more deadly, was grasped at once by recklessness and despair. Before the time of James II. the potato had become the symbol and reproach of Ireland. An Irish deputation in that reign was followed about the streets of London by a mob with potatoes stuck on poles. Planted without exertion, incapable of being long stored, and liable to disease, this fatal root seemed made for the purpose of covering a grazing country with a population greater than even a corn country could support, training them to improvidence, and at last plunging them in famine.

Even the check which the want of habitations and the expense incurred by the landlord in building them might have imposed, was here wanting. The Irish peasantry themselves built their wretched hovels with materials which lay ready to their hands. Thus there were houses, or rather styes, for as many of them as could live. At the same time eviction, when it took place, was rendered more cruel to them by the feeling that the hovels from which they were evicted, being their own work, were in some sense their own.

Early in the eighteenth century a great murrain among the cattle on the Continent caused the price of Irish cattle to rise, and grazing land to become more valuable. Large grazing farms were then formed in many places, and cotters were evicted from their potato-grounds to make room for them. Lord Charlemont and other patriots speak of this as oppression. But Political Economy would hold that the landlords in this instance carried into effect the behests of nature, and that they did the best thing for the whole community, by turning the land to the most valuable purpose. Morality, however, would require Political Economy to observe that the cotters are the landlord's fellow-men and fellow-Christians, not mere material obstacles to his improvements; and that they are not to be cleared away from the soil on which they live, and which their labour and that of their class has made fruitful, without regard to their subsequent fate, like so many stumps grubbed up to make way for the plough.

This tide of want and misery not only filled Ireland to the brim, but overflowed into England; and, bringing pauperism and disease into our great cities, punished England for whatever share she may have had in Irish wrongs, and compelled her to pay attention to the state of the Irish people.

Strange to say, the Protestant population of Ireland itself began to be thrust out by this ghastly avenger. The Catholic peasantry, clinging with desperate tenacity to the soil, outbid the Protestants for the holdings. The landlords, in their blind cupidity, caught at the advance in rent; and they moreover, like the degenerate English of the Pale in former times, preferred Catholic serfs to Protestant tenants[t]. The Protestants emigrated to America. The Catholics who had ousted them paid the rent for a time by working the land to exhaustion; and the evil was thus made continually worse. So completely was agricultural improvement arrested, that in 1858, when a considerable change for the better had

[t] See Phelan's Remains, vol. ii. p. 42.

taken place in every respect, M. de Lavergne calculated that an expenditure of more than thirty millions would still be required to bring Ireland to the agricultural level of the sister island. This loss, now that the two islands are united and all their interests are in common, falls of course equally on the whole empire.

The famine of 1846 was the most terrible of Irish famines, and the most momentous in its consequences, but it was not the first. In 1741 a person resident in Ireland wrote:—" Having been absent from this country some years, on my return to it last summer, I found it the most miserable scene of distress that I ever read of in history. Want and misery on every face, the rich unable to relieve the poor, the roads spread with dead and dying bodies; mankind the colour of the docks and nettles which they fed on; two or three, sometimes more, on a car, going to the grave, for want of bearers to carry them, and many buried only in the fields and ditches where they perished. The universal scarcity was followed by fluxes and malignant fevers, which swept off multitudes of all sorts, so that whole villages were laid waste." He reckons the mortality, vaguely, at 400,000 [u]. Berkeley also, in his Address to the Catholic clergy, speaks of this terrible famine, as well as of the general wretchedness of the people.

We have seen that in Swift's time some of these wretched beings sold themselves to the Barbadoes. Multitudes enlisted in the army: it is reckoned that at one time two-fifths of the forces of the empire were Irish-

---

[u] Abstract of a pamphlet called "The Groans of Ireland," Gentleman's Magazine, vol. xi. p. 638.

men. Those who desire to maintain large standing armies may learn from history that misery is the great recruiting-sergeant, and that the only cheap recruiting ground is among a degraded and despairing people. Not only the British army was filled with Irish; they enlisted in great numbers in the armies of France and Spain. The French Abbé M. Geoghehan, in his History of Ireland, dedicated to the Irish troops in the service of France, states that "from calculations and researches made at the French war-office," it has been ascertained, that from the arrival of the Irish troops in France in 1691 up to 1745, the year of the battle of Fontenoy, more than 450,000 Irishmen died in the service of France. The number staggers belief: but it is held not to be incredible by Newenham in his work on Irish population. People pay for the blood of mercenaries, and they use it. This consumption of the Irish people in mercenary war, however, is the least hideous item of the hideous account. Death on the field of battle, though in an alien cause, is happiness compared with death by famine or by plague.

But notwithstanding these outlets the island became utterly overcharged. A mortal struggle for existence between the cotters on the one side, and the middlemen and tithe-proctors on the other commenced; and a century of agrarian conspiracy and crime was the result. The atrocities perpetrated by the Whiteboys, especially in the earlier period of agrarianism, (for they afterwards grew somewhat less inhuman,) are such as to make the flesh creep. No language can be too strong in speaking of the horrors of such a state of society.

But it would be unjust to confound these agrarian conspiracies with ordinary crime, or to suppose that they imply a propensity to ordinary crime either on the part of those who commit them, or on the part of the people who connive at and favour their commission. In the districts where agrarian conspiracy and outrage were most rife, the number of ordinary crimes was very small. In Munster, in 1833, out of 973 crimes, 627 were Whiteboy or agrarian, and even of the remainder, many, being crimes of violence, were probably committed from the same motive [y].

In plain truth, the secret tribunals which administered the Whiteboy code were to the people the organs of a wild law of social morality, by which on the whole the interest of the peasant was protected. They were not regular tribunals: neither were the secret tribunals of Germany in the middle ages, the existence of which, and the submission of the people to their jurisdiction, implied the presence of much violence, but not of much depravity, considering the wildness of the times. The Whiteboys "found in their favour already existing a general and settled hatred of the law among the great body of the peasantry [z]." We have seen how much the law, and the ministers of the law, had done to deserve the peasant's love. We have seen, too, in what successive guises property had presented itself to his mind; first as open rapine, then as robbery carried on through the roguish technicalities of an alien code, finally as legalized and systematized oppression. Was

[y] Sir G. C. Lewis, On Irish Disturbances, p. 97. [z] Lewis, p. 250.

it possible that he should have formed so affectionate a reverence either for law or property as would be proof against the pressure of starvation?

So little had the peasantry enjoyed the common training of civilization, that while they were shooting middlemen and tithe-proctors for raising rents and exacting tithes, they were killing each other in faction fights, which, as was before intimated, were a remnant of the old clan system; a proof that the most primitive barbarism had never been fairly left behind. Magistrates are accused of having taken part with these factions, and encouraged this fighting, with a view to turn the violence of the people from themselves upon one another[a]. One witness before the Committee of the House of Commons had "heard gentlemen of the county and magistrates say that it was a good sign to see the lower classes at war with each other, for then it was not to be supposed that they were combining against the State."

It has been clearly proved that these conspiracies and outrages were agrarian, not religious. As the class of landlords happened to be mainly Protestants, while the peasants were mainly Catholics, the difference of religion gave a tinge to the disturbances, and added to their virulence, but it was in no degree their source[b]. The Roman Catholic clergy, as a body, were perfectly blameless; not only so, but in spite of the terrible temptations to play the demagogue under which they were placed by the iniquity of the Code, they arrayed themselves on the side of law. Their own dues

[a] Lewis, p. 289.   [b] Lewis, p. 138, and the following pages.

were, in fact, sometimes the object of attack, as well as the tithes of the Protestant parsons.

Particular odium has been cast on the clergy and their tithe-proctors. It is, indeed, not easy to imagine St. Paul seizing for tithe the goods of a famished peasant belonging to a different religion. But the whole responsibility of the exaction must be held to fall on the State which establishes the Church of the minority. Each of the individual clergymen had as good a right to his tithes as the landlord to his rent; and if he had not taken them, he would have starved. The resistance of the landlords to the payment of tithe of agistment tended to throw the clergy more than ever on the potato grounds of the poor.

The moral degradation arising from this vast mass of helotage could not fail to affect the bearing even of the upper classes of Ireland. It produced in them that want of self-respect and respect for their country in their intercourse with the English which drew from Johnson the bitter remark, "The Irish, Sir, are a very candid people; they never speak well of each other."

One virtue alone could grow in such a soil, that of desperate and almost demoniac courage. In the course of these disturbances, though at a somewhat later period than that of which we are now speaking, a party of Whiteboys entered a house in which were a man, his wife, and their daughter, a little girl. The three were all together in the same room. The ruffians rushed into the room, dragged the man out of the house, and there proceeded to murder him. In the room where the woman and the girl remained, there was a closet with a hole in its door, through which a person placed inside could see into the room. The woman concealed the little girl in this closet, and said to her, "Now, child, they are murdering your father down-stairs, and when they have murdered him, they will come up here and murder me. Take care that, while they are doing it, you look well at them, and mind you swear to them when you see them in the court. I will throw turf on the fire the last thing to give you light, and struggle hard that you may have time to take a good view." The little girl looked in through the hole in the closet-door while her mother was being murdered: she marked the murderers well: she swore to them when she saw them in a court of justice; and they were convicted on her evidence.

Meantime, a momentous change was coming over the world. After the conclusion of the great religious wars, and the overthrow of Louis XIV., comparative peace ensued, reflection commenced, science advanced, philosophy gained power, a strong current of feeling adverse to war and tyranny set in, the fires of the Inquisition slowly sank into ashes, and fanaticism gave place to toleration, which, after what had passed, was too naturally accompanied by indifference to religion. A new set of ideas gained ground, and took hold even on the occupants of despotic thrones, till, unhappily for the world, the movement came to a violent crisis among the nation least capable of directing it to a good issue, and ended in disaster for a time through the crimes and follies of the French Revolution.

In Ireland the spirit of the new era made its first appearance in the person of Chesterfield, who came over as Viceroy to keep the kingdom quiet in 1745, and played the beneficent despot, curbing jobbery, fostering such elements of prosperity as he could find, and treating the Catholics with a philosophic mildness, which left among them a grateful recollection of his reign. His habit of free-thinking made him scorn that political superstition of Ireland, the belief in perpetual plots: and being told by a zealous alarmist that all Connaught was rising, he looked at his watch, and said, "It is past nine, and time for us all to rise." His clear eye, which in France discerned beforehand the coming Revolution, enabled him also to read the true state of the case in Ireland. "Poverty," he observed, "not Popery, was the thing most to be feared." Yet, like Bolingbroke and other statesmen of his cynical school, he had no objection to passing persecuting laws for political purposes. He strongly upheld the "gavel Act" as the means of breaking up the estates of Papists; and two evil Statutes on the subject of marriages between Papists and Protestants, or by Popish priests, dated from his reign.

In 1778, the increasing spirit of toleration began sensibly to exert its power. A Catholic Relief Bill, repealing the more atrocious articles of the Penal Code, was passed first by the English and then by the Irish Parliament. Another beneficent spirit closely akin to toleration, began to make its kind influence felt at the same time. Peace had produced a better feeling between nations, and wiser views of their mutual interests.

In 1776 appeared the "Wealth of Nations." In 1778 Lord North proposed (somewhat under duress, it is true) large relaxations of the iniquitous and absurd restrictions on Irish trade: but the spirit of Protection was still too strong, the light of the coming day had not yet sufficiently spread, and the great boon of emancipation which the Government proposed was cut down to a niggard dole. Two years afterwards the same Minister, taught wisdom by his American disasters, proposed and carried further concessions. Twenty years more, and Mr. Pitt, having come into power instinct with all the liberal ideas of the new era, extinguished one source of misery and discord by giving Ireland a full measure of Free Trade as an article of the Union.

It was in the insurrection of the American Colonies that the great movement of the eighteenth century first assumed a violent and revolutionary form. That event at once deeply affected the politics of Ireland. The Opposition in the Irish Parliament had, since the middle of the century, been gradually growing active and strong. While the terrors of civil war and the proscriptions remained fresh, to suppress the Catholics was the one great object of all the Irish Protestants; and to secure the support of England for that purpose, they had quietly acquiesced in the Statute of George I. which riveted and completed Poynings' law, by declaring that the Parliament of Great Britain had full power to legislate for Ireland. But, as this panic became allayed, and as fanaticism began somewhat to abate, the Irish Opposition turned from the multiplication of measures for the oppression and degradation of the Catholics, to objects of a more respectable and popular kind, such as the reform of Parliament, and the removal of the restrictions on trade. In the case of America, the Irish patriots saw the counterpart of their own. It was that of a colony on which the mother-country had imposed commercial restrictions for her own imagined advantage, which she had assumed to treat in all things as a dependency, and which had resisted her tyrannical pretensions and declared itself a nation. They were fired by the example. Under colour of raising a volunteer force to resist a French invasion, they rose virtually in armed insurrection; held a military convention of a revolutionary character; wrung from the English Government, enfeebled and intimidated by the American disaster, the repeal of Poynings' Act, and of the supplementary Act of George I., which formed the two links of the legislative dependency; and made Ireland, saving her allegiance to the British Crown, an independent nation. The year 1782 may be considered as that of the Irish Revolution; a revolution which formed an intermediate part of the train which was first fired in America, and ended with the great explosion in France.

The Irish patriots who accomplished this revolution could not fail to set a high value on the work of their own hands. "I found Ireland on her knees," cried Grattan; "I watched over her with an eternal solicitude; I have traced her progress from injuries to arms, and from arms to liberty. Spirit of Swift, spirit of Molyneux, your genius has prevailed! Ireland is now a nation! In that new character I hail her! And, bowing to her august presence, I say, *Esto perpetua.*" An arrangement which involved the existence of two legislatures under one Crown, yet independent of each other, and legislating separately, on matters not only of internal policy but of peace and war, for one empire, was obviously untenable, and destined to end either in complete separation, or, as it eventually did, in a complete Union. Yet it is perhaps to be lamented that the provisional agency of an independent Irish Parliament was not prolonged. For the patriot party in it were led, some by their liberal and generous temper, and all by the necessities of their position, to make common cause with the mass of the Irish people. They took the first step towards the political emancipation of the Catholics, by restoring to them the elective franchise. They might have pressed with effect the admission of Catholics to Parliament. They might have been drawn even into dealing a blow against religious ascendancy: and thus the Irish people, like the Scotch people, might have come into the Union with England on perfectly fair and equal terms, and the Irish Union, like the Scotch Union, might have been final, complete, and happy.

To believe that the mere possession of a Parliament of her own was the source, as is alleged, of a glorious flood of prosperity to Ireland, would be to attribute a magic virtue indeed to parliamentary institutions. From an inquiry made for the instruction of the English Government in 1784 into the composition of this beneficent and august assembly, it appeared that of the three hundred seats one hundred and sixteen were shared among five-and-twenty proprietors, one nobleman having sixteen to his own share; and that Government could count on eighty-six votes of members for proprietary seats, the owners of which let them out for titles, places, or pensions, twelve votes of their own, forty-five votes of placemen, and thirty-two of gentlemen who had promises, or had avowed their expectations[c]. The system of Irish government after the declaration of Independence probably became more profligate than ever: the Castle contended with its increased difficulties by an increase of bribery; the country, nominally independent, was, in fact, a dependency governed by corruption and intrigue; and these times contributed their full share to the formation of that class of Irish jobbers, place-hunters, and intriguers which long survived the Union, and will not be extinguished till the last trace of Ascendancy is gone, and Government rests firmly on its true foundations—equal justice, and the welfare of the whole people. "I have settled the business of Chancellor of the Order of St. Patrick," says the Duke of Wellington, when Chief Secretary for Ireland. "He will have *literally the copper collars*, for they are of copper. Mr. ——, the father of the ——, stole the money for the gold collars and bought copper." This gallant effort on the part of some zealous servant of the Government, as no doubt the unnamed person was, to stem the tide of disaffection and support loyalty and Protestantism, is coarser in form, but not baser in substance, than the system of corruption by means of peerages, places, and pensions,

[c] See Massey's History of England, vol. iii. p. 264.

by which the Government majority in the Irish Parliament was ordinarily held together, and which, the enthusiastic burst of 1782 once over, seems to have triumphed pretty steadily over the impediments thrown in its way by patriot virtue.

Hallam says of the great Parliamentary period of Irish history, that it was "a period fruitful of splendid eloquence, and of ardent, though always uncompromising patriotism." This praise, perhaps, is at least sufficiently high. The orators of the Irish Parliament lived for the most part in a society which was a whirl of reckless gaiety and conviviality, alternating with barbarous duels and ghastly suicides. They did not change their natures when they entered the political arena; and the Irish Debates bore a strong resemblance to an Irish drinking-bout of the more brilliant kind. It is difficult to believe that there was in that assembly the wisdom which founds lasting institutions and saves a nation. Grattan stood among his associates without a peer. In him, if in any one of the Irish patriots, good sense and moral dignity were to be found. Yet it is sometimes difficult to distinguish his eloquence from the rant which betrays great want of sense, or his invective from the ribaldry which betrays a want of moral dignity. It is a pregnant fact, when we are estimating the worth of a political assembly, that its foremost man, even in mature life, and when translated to the colder and more critical sphere of the English House of Commons, could say of Napoleon's march to Moscow:—"Ambition is omnivorous; it feasts on famine, and sheds tons of blood that it may starve on ice, in order to commit a robbery on desolation [d]." And it is a fact not less pregnant that he could speak in debate of an opponent's "broken beak," in allusion to his broken nose. No doubt the foolery of the Irish Parliament was good fun. The fools of English Parliaments are not so amusing as Sir Boyle Roche, who among many strokes of humour, said, in replying to a member who had protested against burdening posterity by a loan :—" What, Mr. Speaker! and so we are to beggar ourselves for fear of vexing posterity! Now I would ask the honourable gentleman, and this *still more* honourable House, why we should put ourselves out of the way to do anything for *posterity* :—for what has *posterity* done for us." A roar of laughter following, Sir Boyle, apprehending that he had been misunderstood, begged leave to explain " that by *posterity* he did not at all mean our *ancestors*, but those who were to come *immediately* after *them*."

To preserve the picture of these times for the benefit of the historian, fortune placed Sir Jonah Barrington in a good social, legal, and parliamentary position. Nature had kindly made him without reticence or shame. Nothing in his "Sketches" is more incredible than some things which are certainly true, such as the catalogue of duels fought by eminent legal and official personages, in which figure the Lord Chancellor, three Chief Justices, several Judges, and the Provost of the University of Dublin. The duelling code, under which these worthies fought, "was settled at Clonmel assizes (1777), by the gentlemen delegates of Tipperary,

---

[d] See the character of Grattan in Lord Stanhope's History, ch. lxv.

Galway, Mayo, Sligo, and Roscommon, and prescribed for general adoption throughout Ireland^e."

Mr. Pitt's early policy towards Ireland was liberal in every sense. He at once prepared to give her free trade with England. He attempted to give her, as well as England, Parliamentary Reform. He founded Maynooth. There can be no doubt that he desired a broad measure of Catholic Emancipation. He had admitted the Catholics of Canada to full political rights under a free constitution. After this there was, in fact, no more to be said. But the liberal policy of Mr. Pitt, like the liberal policy of continental reformers, was fatally arrested, and the world was flung into dismay, despair of liberty, and absolutist reaction, by the tremendous eruption of absurdity, cruelty, and ultimately of military vanity and rapacity, which Frenchmen imagine to be the grandest and most beneficent event in history. The march of reform both in England and Ireland was cut short: the moderate party among the reformers passed at once, or within a short time, from the camp of progress to that of its opponents. But the attempt of the more violent party to follow the example of their allies the Jacobins, while it flashed in the pan in England, involved Ireland in the flames first of foreign invasion and then of a horrible civil war.

This revolutionary movement bore an analogy to the movement of 1641, inasmuch as it commenced not with the Catholic masses, but with the Republicans of Belfast, who were for the most part Protestants or Deists, and among whom the conspiracy of the United Irish-

[e] Barrington's Sketches, vol. ii. p. 14. He gives the code *in extenso*.

men took its rise. Most of these men were not in any respect above the average level of the French Jacobin Club. Lord Edward Fitzgerald seems to have been merely a weak, hot-headed enthusiast; a crack-brained Prelate-Peer, the Earl of Bristol, Bishop of Derry, took the part of the Duke of Orleans, and played Egalité to the Irish Sansculottes. The only man of real mark in the party was Wolfe Tone. Tone was not a first-class man of action, but he was a first-rate man of the second class; brave, adventurous, sanguine, fertile in resource, buoyant under misfortune, warm-hearted, and capable of winning, if not of commanding men. Though his name is little known among Englishmen, he was near being almost as fatal an enemy to England as Hannibal was to Rome.

Mainly through the perseverance, insinuation, and address of this obscure envoy, the French Directory were induced to send forth the great armament of Hoche, which appeared in Bantry Bay, and would certainly have effected its landing, but for obstacles of wind and weather, such as steam has now annulled. After the failure of Hoche's expedition, another great armament was fitted out in the Texel, where it long lay ready to come forth, while the English fleet, the only safeguard of our coasts, was crippled by the mutiny at the Nore. But the wind once more fought for England, and the Batavian fleet came out at last only to be destroyed at Camperdown. Tone was personally engaged in both expeditions, and his lively Diary, the image of his character, gives us vivid accounts of both. The third effort of the French Government was feeble, and ended in the futile landing of a small force under Humbert. Their main strength had been drawn away to Egypt by Bonaparte, who loved neither the projects of Hoche nor Republicans, and who is asserted to have said to the Directory, when a further effort on behalf of the Irish was under discussion, "What more do you desire from the Irish? You see that their movements already operate a powerful diversion [f]." The words, if they were really spoken, are instructive.

In the last expedition Tone himself was taken prisoner, and, having been condemned to death, committed suicide in prison. Some difficulty arose between the authorities on the occasion, and the passions of those times were fierce enough to give colour to a suspicion that his enemies wished to place the halter round the mangled neck of the dying man. It was well for Ireland, as well as for England, that Tone failed in his enterprise. Had he succeeded, his country would for a time have been treated as Switzerland and the Batavian Republic were treated by their French regenerators, and, in the end, it would have been surely reconquered and punished by the power which was mistress of the sea. He had himself, when embarking with the French army of liberation at Brest, the pleasure of seeing "a little army of commissaries, who were going to Ireland to make their fortunes [g]." He promised himself that he would keep his eye on these gentlemen; and if he had, he would have found that they did not subsist solely on "fraternity" or "ideas." But now that all is over, we can afford to say that Tone gallantly ventured his

[f] Life of Wolfe Tone, vol. ii. p. 514.   [g] Ibid., vol. ii. p. 276.

life in what naturally appeared to him, and would to a high-spirited Englishman under the same circumstances have appeared, a good cause. One of his race had but too much reason then to "hate the very name of England," and to look forward to the burning of her cities with feelings in which pity struggled with revenge for mastery, but revenge prevailed [h]. Nor can we help feeling the justice of his sarcasm when he says, in his address to the people of Ireland, "to compensate you for the loss of your independent existence as a nation: for the destruction of your trade and manufactures, the plunder of your property, the interdiction of education to three-fourths of your people, and their absolute exclusion from a state of political existence, you have been gravely told that you participated in what is called, in the cant of your enemies, *the inestimable blessings of the British Constitution.*"

From the Republicans the disturbance spread, as in 1641, to that mass of blind disaffection and hatred, national, social, agrarian, and religious, which was always smouldering among the Catholic peasantry. With these sufferers the political theories of the French Revolutionists had no influence; they looked to French invasion, as well as to domestic insurrection, merely as a deliverance from the oppression under which they groaned. So far were they from being propagators of the ideas which advanced with the Tricolor, that in their coarse ballads they sang of the French banner which was to be displayed beside the Harp of Ireland

---

[h] Tone's Life, vol. ii. p. 241.

as the banner of the Fleur-de-Lys[i]. Nor, though the same ballads breathed hatred against "tyrant heretics," was the "heresy" of the upper classes the cause of the outbreak, but the "tyranny" of race and caste with which the heresy happened to be associated. The leading Roman Catholics, both clerical and lay, were on the side of the government. The mass of the Catholic priesthood were well inclined to take the same side. They could have no sympathy with an Atheist Republic, red with the blood of priests, as well as with the blood of a son of St. Louis. If some of the order were concerned in the movement, it was as demagogues, sympathizing with their peasant brethren, not as priests. Yet the Protestants insisted on treating the Catholic clergy as rebels by nature. They had assuredly done their best to make them so. The judicial assassination of Father Sheeby, a popular priest, for alleged complicity in the murder of a man whose body never was found, and who was proved by witnesses of good character to have left the kingdom, may be pronounced to have been as foul as any of the assassinations committed in the courts of Scraggs or Jeffreys[k].

No sooner did the Catholic peasantry begin to move and organize themselves than the Protestant gentry and yeomanry as one man became Cromwellians again. Then commenced a Reign of Terror scarcely less savage than that of the Jacobins, against whom Europe was in

[i] "The fleur-de-lys and harp we'll display
While tyrant heretics shall mould to clay."

[k] See Madden's "United Irishmen," Irish Series, ch. ii.; and Lewis On Irish Disturbances, p. 14.

arms, as a hideous and portentous brood of evil, the scourge and horror of the whole human race. The suspected conspirators were intimidated, and confessions, or pretended confessions, were extorted by loosing upon the homes of the peasantry the license and barbarity of an irregular soldiery more cruel than a regular invader. Flogging, half-hanging, pitch-capping, picketing, went on over a large district, and the most barbarous scourgings, without trial, were inflicted in the Riding-house at Dublin, in the very seat of government and justice. This was styled, "exerting a vigour beyond the law;" and to become the object of such vigour, it was enough, as under Robespierre, to be suspected of being suspect.

No one has yet fairly undertaken the revolting but salutary task of writing a faithful and impartial history of that period; but from the accounts we have, it appears not unlikely that the peasantry, though undoubtedly in a disturbed state, and to a great extent secretly organized, might have been kept quiet by measures of lenity and firmness; and that they were gratuitously scourged and tortured into open rebellion.

When they did rebel, they shewed, as they had shewn in 1641, what the galley-slave is when, having long toiled under the lash, he contrives in a storm to slip his chains and become master of the vessel. The atrocities of Wexford and Vinegar-Hill rivalled the atrocities of Portnadown. Nor when the rebellion was vanquished did the victors fail to renew the famous feats of Sir Charles Coote and of the regiment of Cole. We now possess terrible and overwhelming evidence of their sanguinary ferocity in the correspondence of Lord Cornwallis, who was certainly no friend to rebels, having fought against them in America, but who was a man of sense and heart, most wisely sent over to quench the insurrection, and pacify the country. In one place, after stating that the overt rebellion is declining, he proceeds to dwell on the horrors of a state of martial law administered by Irishmen, heated with passion and revenge. "But all this," he says, "is trifling, compared to the numberless murders that are hourly committed by our people without any process or examination whatever. The yeomanry are in the style of the Loyalists in America, only much more numerous and powerful, and a thousand times more ferocious. These men have served their country, but they now take the lead in rapine and murder. The Irish militia, with few officers, and those chiefly of the worst kind, follow closely on the heels of the yeomanry in murder and every kind of atrocity; and the fencibles take a share, although much behind-hand with the others. . . . The conversation of the principal persons of the country all tends to encourage this system of blood; and the conversation, even at my table, where, you will suppose, I do all I can to prevent it, always turns on hanging, shooting, burning, &c. And if a priest has been put to death, the greatest joy is expressed by the whole company. So much for Ireland and my wretched situation[1]." In another letter he says, "The accounts that you see of the numbers of the enemy destroyed in every action, are, I conclude, greatly exaggerated: from my

[1] Cornwallis Correspondence, vol. ii. p. 371.

own knowledge of military affairs, I am sure that a very small proportion of them only could be killed in battle; and I am much afraid that any man in a brown coat who is found within several miles of the field of action is butchered without discrimination[m]." And again, that it may not be supposed that the lust of butchery was confined to yeomanry and fencibles, or to individual fanatics and ruffians, he says, "The principal persons of this country, and the members of both Houses of Parliament, are, in general, averse to all acts of clemency, and although they do not express, and perhaps are too much heated to see the ultimate effects which their violence must produce, would pursue measures that could only terminate in the extirpation of the greater number of the inhabitants, and in the utter destruction of the country[n]." Such were the members of both houses of that Parliament which is imagined to have showered so many blessings on the people!

A party of yeomanry were patrolling at night. They entered a cabin occupied by a woman and her son, who was taking his supper. One of the yeomanry charged the youth with having been a rebel, and declared he would shoot him. The youth begged for his life, saying that he was ready to go before a magistrate. The trooper twice snapped his piece at him, and another of the party coming in, fired at him and broke his arm, though the mother, seeing their murderous intentions, tried to seize the muzzle of the gun. As the youth lay wounded on the floor, the first trooper deliberately took aim at him, and shot him dead. The murderer

[m] p. 357. [n] p. 360.

was brought before a permanent court-martial then sitting at Dublin, and presided over by a nobleman. The facts were not denied, but the defence was that the murdered youth had been a rebel, though at the time of his murder provided with a protection, and that the murderer was a very loyal subject. To prove this some evidence was tendered, and, though mostly hearsay, admitted. The Court "found that the prisoner did shoot and kill Thomas Dogherty, a rebel, but acquitted him of any malicious or wilful intention of murder." Lord Cornwallis saved the honour of the English Government by publicly expressing his disapprobation of the sentence, as an acquittal of a prisoner "who appeared by the clearest evidence to have been guilty of a cruel and deliberate murder," dissolved the Court, and inflicted on the murderer the only punishment in his power, by ordering that he should not be admitted to any corps of yeomanry in the kingdom°. If Burke had then been living he might have found in the mother of Thomas Dogherty almost as good a subject for a rhapsody as in Marie Antoinette. Lord Cornwallis was much blamed by thorough-going Loyalists for discouraging loyalty on this occasion.

This is stated to have been by no means a solitary case. Lord Cornwallis took the opinion of the Attorney-General as to the possibility of bringing to another trial an officer who had committed a murder of the same kind, but had been acquitted by a Loyalist court-martial, in the teeth of clear evidence of his guilt. The court-martial in this case found some of the party

° Cornwallis Correspondence, vol. ii. p. 421.

who had accompanied the officer guilty; but recommended them to mercy on the ground that "at the time when the crime was committed, they did not think that they were doing an improper act in putting a person *that they thought a rebel* to death." Every subterfuge, in the way of rejecting legal and admitting illegal evidence, is said to have been resorted to by courts-martial to avoid giving honest decisions on these occasions [p].

The evidence of Lord Cornwallis is of course the best. But the charges of cruelty and brutality against the Loyalists, which are authenticated by his correspondence, are far from being the worst that have been brought. Besides indiscriminate butchery, and the more than savage use of torture, they are very circumstantially accused of having committed the grossest outrages and barbarities on women, and even of having massacred children [q]. They are accused of having condemned to death by court-martial a boy of fifteen, and of having brought him to be executed at his mother's door [r].

These were the crimes, not of individual ruffians, but of a faction; a faction which must take its place in history besides that of Robespierre, Couthon, and Carrier. Both the Orangemen and the Jacobins may plead that a long series of antecedent circumstances had conspired to make them what they were; and that a fatal crisis had occurred to bring out in their worst form the

---

[p] Cornwallis Correspondence, vol. ii. p. 423.
"United Irishmen," First Series, pp. 292—364.
[q] See Madden's
[r] Ibid., p. 337.

evil qualities which an unhappy training had produced. The murders and other atrocities committed by the Jacobins were more numerous than those committed by the Orangemen, and as the victims were of higher rank they excited more indignation and pity; but in the use of torture the Orangemen seem to have reached a pitch of fiendish cruelty which was scarcely attained by the Jacobins. Both factions might plead the wretched excuse of extreme peril and maddening fear; but the danger of invasion by the armies of the Coalition, which brought on the diabolical delirium of the Jacobins, was greater than the danger to which the Orangemen were exposed: and the Jacobin party was almost entirely composed of men taken from the lowest of the people, whereas among the Irish terrorists were found men of high social position and good education. It must be added that the ferocity of the Jacobins was in a slight degree redeemed by their fanaticism. Their objects were not entirely selfish. They murdered aristocrats, not only because they hated and feared them, but because they wildly imagined them to stand in the way of the social and political millennium, which, according to Rousseau, awaited the acceptance of mankind.

Those who took part, on either side, in the atrocities of 1798, have long ago been summoned to answer for their misdeeds to a Justice compared with which the best-informed and calmest judgments of history are but ignorance and passion. No man now living can sincerely feel that he is called upon, in any way whatever, to avenge a cause which has passed entirely into the hands of God. It would be wickedness or madness to allow the recollection of these events to influence a single action in the present day, except in so far as it is necessary to make allowance for the social and political difficulties which have been left behind, and to remember that after a terrible storm, though the wind may have abated, the waves will long continue to run high. Happily, among the mass of the people on whom these calamities chiefly fell, the memory of wrong is shortlived; tradition, their only record, fades away in one or two generations; and no accusing monuments rise above the turf that clothes their graves. If the annals of past feuds and wrongs are preserved, it must be by literary men, who can seldom have suffered personally by the crimes which they relate; and whose only object in recalling the horrors of 1798 ought to be to guard the nation for the future against the spirit of faction, always murderous in thought, and capable, if a strong temptation presents itself, of becoming murderous in deed.

Among the phantoms of hatred and suspicion which arose from this field of carnage, was the horrible idea that the English Government had intentionally stimulated the Irish people into rebellion in order to pave the way for the Union. No evidence in support of this charge can be produced. But it certainly concerns those who undertake the defence of Mr. Pitt's honour to prove very distinctly either that he was not cognizant of the atrocities which were being committed by his party in Ireland, or that he vigorously repressed and manfully condemned them. The appointment of so humane a man as Lord Cornwallis to the Viceroyalty at the moment when humanity was most required, is undoubtedly a great point in the Minister's favour, but it is not sufficient of itself to clear his name.

The Reign of Terror in 1798 was at all events destined to be the last exhibition, on a great scale, of uncontrolled Ascendancy. The Rebellion, by striking terror into the separatist party among the Irish Protestants had, as a matter of fact, the effect of rendering possible a measure by which the two portions of the empire were at last blended into one people, every part of which shares fully in the safeguards provided by public opinion and free institutions for the whole.

There can be no doubt that the Union was carried through the Irish Parliament partly by corrupt means. We can gather from the correspondence of Lord Cornwallis how repulsive the task imposed upon him as negotiator for the English Government on this occasion must have been to his honourable mind. Of the men with whom he had to deal, he says, " I do not flatter myself with the hope of obtaining any very disinterested opinion upon the subject on this side of the water, as I have not the smallest doubt that every man whom I might consult, would advise such measures as he thought would best suit his private views, without having the smallest consideration for the public welfare[a]." The consent of the Irish Parliament was necessary in order to carry a measure of vital importance to both nations; and as the Irish Parliament were

[a] Correspondence, vol. ii. p. 258.

venal, it was necessary to purchase their consent. If the conduct of Government was not pure, neither perhaps will it be reckoned among the most unpardonable instances of corruption. The benefits of the measure to the present generation are not in any degree tainted by the means employed in removing an obstruction from its path sixty years ago. If any question as to a byegone transaction can be rationally raised at the present time, it is not whether the Union was approved by the corrupt and selfish oligarchy which styled itself the Irish Parliament, but whether it was approved or acquiesced in by those who might fairly be considered the best representatives of the Irish people. On this point we have pretty good evidence. There can be no doubt that Lord Cornwallis, in his confidential correspondence with his Government, desired to inform them with perfect accuracy of the state of feeling in Ireland as to the proposed Union, and the amount of resistance which they would have to overcome. He expressly states that "there appears no indisposition on the part of the leading Catholics," but that, "on the contrary, he believes they will consider any transfer of power from their opponents as a boon;" and while he predicts opposition, on commercial grounds, at Dublin, he holds out sanguine hopes of support on the same grounds in the great Catholic cities of Limerick and Cork[1]. The consent of the Catholic clergy, so far as that body did consent, must be held to have been vitiated, since hopes of an arrangement in their favour were held out to them, and not fulfilled.

[1] Correspondence, vol. ii. p. 447.

It may be readily granted that unless the Union was for the good of both parties, it was for the good of neither. A nation must be very shallow or very depraved which, in the meridian light of modern philosophy, can imagine that a mere extension of its territory, unsanctioned by nature and morality, can add to its greatness. Greatness in nations, as well as in men, is a moral quality, from which immoral acquisitions must detract in reality, though they may add to it in appearance. An alien and disaffected element incorporated in a nation can only be a source of internal division and weakness. It would be better in every point of view, that the British Empire should be reduced to a single island, to England alone, to Yorkshire or Kent, than that it should include anything which is not really its own.

It would have been as difficult for O'Connell to renounce the excitement, not to mention the profits, of his occupation as an agitator, as it is for a successful opera-singer to renounce the excitement of her calling; and it is therefore not wonderful that when Catholic Emancipation had been disposed of, he should have taken up with Repeal. But those, if any there now be, who desire to renew the enterprize in which he totally failed, and which he in truth pursued towards the end of his life with but a half conviction and a faint heart, are bound to consider beforehand, not only how they shall repeal the Union, but what they will do with Ireland when the Union has been repealed. Otherwise they will get out of a harbour which does not suit their predilections, only to find themselves embarked upon a tempestuous and shoreless sea.

There are four relations in which Ireland may be placed with regard to the sister island,—dependency, independence, federation, and union. The relation of dependency has been tried during six centuries, and there are few who would desire to experience it again, as the consequence of a disruption leading to a war and a second conquest of the weaker island by the stronger. Independence would of course be feasible in itself, it it could only be accompanied by geographical separation; but so close a neighbourhood would involve contact, and contact would bring on collision: rivalry, jealousy, hostility would spring up all the more certainly, because there would be between the two countries the memory of a former union, and of a recent divorce; and Ireland, menaced by the power of England, would become the ward and the vassal of France, or some other foreign power, which for its own purposes would constitute itself her protector. The federal relation is natural and useful when it is entered into by several states of tolerably equal power, but it could not be naturally or usefully formed between two states, one of which is far more powerful than the other, since in the Federal Councils the vote of the more powerful would always prevail. There remains only union, and if this alone remains, common-sense requires us heartily to embrace it, and to endeavour, by the abolition of every relic of Ascendancy and ancient misgovernment, to render it perfectly fair, honourable, and beneficial to both nations.

The Repealers themselves, indeed, generally speaking, betray their misgivings as to the soundness of their theory, by not venturing to propose a complete Repeal. What they propose is, if we may be allowed to use an undignified expression, a sort of dog-collar union, in which two distinct nations with independent legislatures, and (as the legislature in a constitutional monarchy is the government) with independent governments, would be linked together by a nominal allegiance to the same Crown. It is idle to argue with any one who cannot himself, on five minutes' reflection, see that such an arrangement must be an irony or a nuisance. Either the allegiance would prove a nullity, and in a short time be formally cast off, or the Parliamentary Government of England would rule the Irish Parliament, as it was ruled during the brief period of its legal independence, by corruption and intrigue.

To settle the external relations of Ireland when the Union had been repealed, would be difficult enough; but to settle her internal constitution would be still more so. As a part of the empire, united to a population which has undergone a long training in the difficult art of self-government, the Irish people are able to support Parliamentary institutions. But would they be able to support them, if they were cast adrift and left to themselves? And yet what other institutions are there to which the nation is accustomed and attached, and which could command its allegiance; an allegiance which, especially in the case of a warm-hearted and imaginative race, the mere demonstration of utility will hardly suffice to secure? Even Parliamentary institutions, after the English model, require a King as their coping-stone. But who is to be the King of Ireland? Where are the restorers of its nationality to look for a royal race to which the hearts of the people may turn? Their search will be vain,—if we may be permitted to indulge in an Hibernicism,— first, because the royal race of Ireland is extinct, and secondly, because it never existed. To find the heir of Roderic O'Connor would be impossible; and if he were found, he would be the heir of a powerful chieftain, exercising an accidental supremacy through his personal power, not of a legitimate king. But suppose an Irish Monarchy established, and the allegiance of the Keltic and Catholic Irish secured to it; there would still remain, driven deep into its flank, the English and Scotch colony, forming a minority indeed in numbers, but a minority which has shewn itself, through the whole course of Irish history, almost a match for the majority in moral and physical power. What sort of element would the Anglican Protestants and Scotch Presbyterians be in a Catholic Parliament, and among the subjects of a Catholic king? Would they not assume at once an attitude of exclusiveness and hostility fatal to the peace and solidity of the State? And if vanquished in the political struggle, would they not throw themselves on the support of their kinsmen and fellow-Protestants in the neighbouring kingdom, form an outpost of England on the Irish soil, and repeat the fatal history of the Pale?

The truth is, that the course of events has left no basis whereon Irish nationality can be established. The only pretext for separation is the narrow channel which runs between the two islands, and which grows narrower with every improvement in steam navigation. Both countries are inhabited by the same mixture of races, the Kelt, the Saxon, and the Norman, with many heterogeneous additions, though the proportions are different in the two cases, the Kelts in Ireland greatly outnumbering the Teutons, while the Teutons in Britain greatly outnumber the Kelts. Look at any list of Repealers, declaiming in favour of Irish nationality and denouncing the Saxon; you are sure to find among them Saxon names, perhaps those of Cromwellians. There is also the same mixture of religion in both countries, though in this case the proportions differ still more widely than in the case of race. But what is of most importance, and in fact almost decisive, the language of both islands is the same. The number of the Irish who still speak Erse alone is a mere fraction of the whole population, and that fraction is fast dwindling away. The strenuous but futile efforts of the Repeal party to galvanize the old national tongue, serve only to shew their sense of the important bearing which its disappearance has on the question of national separation.

To return to Pitt's measure. That measure, however wise and however beneficial in its ultimate effects, could not immediately remedy the evils which had accumulated during six disastrous centuries, and which had been recently aggravated by a terrible civil war. It could not at once allay the resentment of the oppressed, or quell the tyrannical pride of the oppressor. It could not divest names, anniversaries, toasts, party tunes of bitter meanings and bitter associations. It could not confer upon the mass of the people political qualities, the fruits of a political education which fortune had denied them. It could not extirpate at a stroke the inveterate habits of official jobbery and party corruption which the government of a dependency inevitably breeds, and of which the Castle was the immemorial seat. It could not give uprightness, independence, and self-reliance to spirits long subjected to influences the most fatal to those virtues, or inspire with moderation those to whom moderation had long been counted as a crime, and violence on the side of the dominant faction as a virtue. It could not save future statesmen from having to deal with the turbulence of slaves from whose neck the yoke is suddenly taken, and with the discontent of masters suddenly deprived of their slaves.

But besides these general evils, there remained three special evils of the most formidable kind, which were destined long to render Ireland the "difficulty" of English statesmen. These evils were the surplus population, and the agrarian outrages of which the surplus population was the main cause; the law excluding Catholics from Parliament; and the Established Church.

The difficulties of the surplus population and agrarianism were met by the late and very inadequate remedy of Poor Laws, and by the somewhat irrelevant remedy of Coercion Bills. History will, perhaps, hereafter pronounce that statesmen did not thoroughly grasp the nature of the evil with which they had to deal. At least, it would seem that they attempted what was scarcely practicable, if they thought by legislative provisions either to make the grazing districts of Ireland support a swarming population, or to coerce desperate men into starving, and seeing their families starve in peace. Nature at last took the matter into her own hands. She brought upon Ireland a great famine, and pointed out in a decisive manner the simple course of providing, in the first place, for the immediate necessities of the sufferers, and then relaxing the pressure of excessive numbers by emigration on a great scale. Fortunately, English energy and enterprise had provided on the opposite side of the Atlantic a land of hope and plenty for the Irish, while despair and famine were gathering round their own. There the children of the Puritans received the children of their mortal enemies into a happier home. England paid, on the occasion of the Irish famine, a heavy sum in the shape of relief, as the forfeit for her errors; but she has received it back many times over in the repeal of the Corn Laws, to which the Irish famine gave the decisive blow. The torrent of emigration has now probably reduced the population nearly to the point at which plenty and comfort will become attainable, and the moral checks will begin to operate. Their operation will be assisted by the great system of national education. Growing prosperity will diminish the evil of absenteeism, the increase of which, vaguely attributed to the Union by those who regard that measure as the source of all evil, was, as has been said, probably in the main due to the prevalence of a state of misery amidst which it was dreadful to dwell. Crime and agrarian disturbance are passing away in the train of famine and despair; and justice finds no work for her hands in Tipperary. No one who is not interested in keeping up discontent, pretends to doubt that Ireland is rapidly becoming a more prosperous and a happier country. But there are some persons who are interested in keeping up discontent, and the calamitous past has but too surely left them materials for some time to work on. Once, when Europe was disturbed by a momentary resurrection of Jacobinism from the grave of Robespierre, the Irish agitators succeeded in bringing their country to the brink of a civil war. Their failure, in the event, was signal, and shewed, it may reasonably be hoped, that the scale had decisively turned, and that destiny had no more civil wars in store for Ireland. But they will probably long be able to prevent the continuance of such unbroken and secure tranquillity as is requisite in order to encourage a sufficient influx of the now common riches of the empire into its most backward portion, and to raise Ireland to the level of English and Scotch prosperity.

Of the absurdity and iniquity of a Union which excluded three-fourths of the people of one nation, on the ground of their religion, from the common legislature, there is now no need to dwell. It may be regarded as certain that Mr. Pitt was not foolish or unjust enough to contemplate anything of the kind. There can be no doubt that it was his wish and intention to follow up the Union by a measure of Catholic emancipation, giving the Catholics those rights under the British, which he had given them under the Canadian Constitution. The fourth article of the project of Union sent by his cabinet to Lord Cornwallis is, "All members of the United Houses to take the oaths now taken by British members; but such oaths to be subject to such alterations as may be enacted by the United Parliament." It is evident that the oaths, the alteration of which was contemplated, were those which prevented a Roman Catholic from taking his seat. Lord Cornwallis was instructed to shew this paper as a statement of "the ideas of the Administration" to "the friends of Government," as the Union "had become a very general subject of discussion[u]." It does not appear from his correspondence whether any particular use was made of the fourth article.

The obstacle to Emancipation was the conscience of the King, guided by such spiritual advisers as Lord Eldon and the politicians of that school. The Coronation-oath of the King of France, binding him actually to extirpate heresy, was contemptuously swept aside in 1789. The Coronation-oath of the King of England, or his interpretation of it, as it only bound him to treat heretics with flagrant iniquity, was allowed for more than a quarter of a century to stand in the way of a measure demanded by the most urgent necessity of state as well as the most palpable justice. During a great part of that period, England was contending for her independence and for that of the world against Napoleon; and, the Irish Catholics being disaffected, she fought with one arm paralyzed, or rather, with her forces divided against themselves. While in England all citizens were in arms for the defence of a country

[u] Correspondence, vol. ii. p. 436.

to the institutions of which they had reason to be loyal, Sir Arthur Wellesley, charged to report upon the defences of Ireland, assumed that it must be regarded in effect as a hostile country, and held down by force. Yet the loss of military strength was not the worst. The banner which England raised in the name of justice against the common oppressor, was itself sullied by the stain of oppression. It is needless to comment on the irony of fate which gave such power to a George III. The defenders of Mr. Pitt's character are concerned to shew, and they will in all probability be able to shew, that he did not give any pledge, direct or indirect, to the Irish Catholics as an inducement to consent to the Union. If he had done so, the plea of duty to his Sovereign, who required him to carry on the Government of the country, would not avail to save him from condemnation. The first duty which an English statesman owes to his Sovereign and his country is the preservation of his own honour. The very necessity under which the King was placed of claiming Mr. Pitt's services, was an assurance that he would soon be compelled to surrender at discretion. In truth, it was not such men as the Eldons and the Addingtons that could steer the vessel of the State over so wild a sea.

Macaulay expatiates on the calamities which would have followed if, at the Union with Scotland, the Anglican Church of the minority had been established in that country. "One such Church," he says, alluding to Ireland, "is burden enough for the energies of one empire." It is vain to doubt that the time will come when the people of England will seriously ask themselves whether they are bound to impose upon the energies of their empire even one such burden. Perhaps there is no fairer or less invidious mode of determining this question than by fixing our minds on the parallel case of Scotland, and inquiring whether the considerations which led the authors of the Union with Ireland to act differently in this matter from the authors of the Union with Scotland, are still in force. These considerations were the hatred and contempt felt by the mass of English and Scottish Protestants for the Roman Catholics; the persecuting attitude of Roman Catholicism towards Protestantism in other countries; and the apprehension that the profession of the Roman Catholic religion was in some degree inconsistent with loyalty to the State and civil duty. If hatred and contempt for Roman Catholics still linger among the vulgar of all classes, such feelings have long passed away from those minds which, if opinion continues to govern the world, and intellect to lead opinion, will surely determine the sentiments of the next generation. Roman Catholicism has not yet ceased to be persecuting in Spain, and it has only just ceased to be persecuting in Austria; facts of which Roman Catholics, while they complain of the hardship of their own comparatively happy position in Ireland, are bound to take notice. But all wise men have long ceased to imagine that we can advance the cause of toleration in the world by making ourselves accomplices in the practice of persecution. Nothing can afford a shadow of excuse for the state of things existing in Spain, unless it be the state of things existing in Ireland.

Finally, though it would be sophistry to pretend that the Church of Rome had not in past ages terribly justified the fear of her political influence, and though Popes might now be as willing as ever, if they had the power, to step between a Protestant State and the allegiance of its subjects, experience has proved that men are governed in these matters by their real interests, and that they will be good subjects to any Government in the advantages of which they fully share. If there is any disaffection to the State among the Catholics of Ireland, it is because the State still gives them just grounds for disaffection. But even were it otherwise, were it as impossible as the supporters of intolerance pretend, for Roman Catholics to live in political union with Protestants, that would indeed be a strong reason for not forming a political union with a nation of Roman Catholics; but it is no reason for treating them with injustice.

Those whose conduct in this matter is decided more by prejudice than by principle, and whose prejudice rests mainly on traditional fears, will probably be much influenced in favour of a more liberal course by the visible decline of the Papacy and its manifest inability to give effect to the ambitious designs which it once undoubtedly entertained, and is still supposed to entertain. When Elizabeth persecuted Papists, the Papacy wielded not only its own thunderbolts, but the more efficacious arms of the great Catholic monarchies. Of those monarchies, France, the eldest daughter of the Church, has now become the eldest daughter of Voltaire; Austria, if she continues to exist as an empire, is not likely ever again to take part in a crusade; and Spain, though she is gradually putting off her decrepitude, is at the same time gradually putting off her bigotry, and will scarcely renew her attempts to propagate over Europe with arms an authority which she refuses to assist when threatened with destruction in its own consecrated seat. At the same time Italy has thrown off the yoke, and passed, though not in her religious creed, yet in her political sentiments and in sympathies which lie deeper than any formal creed, to the Protestant side. People may still be tempted to maltreat Roman Catholics from bigotry, but the most nervous can scarcely be tempted to maltreat them from fear.

If English statesmen imagined that the Anglican establishment in Ireland would propagate Protestantism, they must by this time be undeceived. Supposing that confidence may be placed in certain indications before mentioned, a spontaneous movement of a Protestant kind among the Irish people is an event by no means out of the question; but the last Church to which they are likely to be converted is that which at once, from the character of its worship, is most opposed to their temperament, and, from its past history and associations is the natural object of their most rooted detestation. Protestantism would in truth stand a far better chance in Ireland if it were not encumbered with this fatal aid. The experiment has now been fairly tried. The impediment placed in the way of Anglicanism by the difference of language has been removed, English being now almost universally spoken by the people. The enervating hour of secure ascendancy having passed away, and the energies of the Irish clergy having been stimulated by peril, they have probably for some time been doing all that the clergy of an Establishment can reasonably be expected to do. It is impossible that the patronage of a State Church should ever be exercised wholly without regard to political motives; but the special abuse of Irish Church patronage appears to have ceased, so that in this respect also the Church has of late years had fair play. The result, as shewn by the religious census for Ireland, is not doubtful. The hold of the Irish Establishment on the religious affections of the Irish people is a garrison of twenty thousand men. At that price England purchases a source of just discontent and perpetual disaffection. At that price she makes the national clergy of Ireland demagogues, and the national religion of Ireland an enemy to social harmony, to political tranquillity, and to the unity of the Empire. At that price she draws upon herself just opprobrium and constant peril. Those who think that this will go on for ever must either have formed a singular estimate of the tendencies of the age or expect that those tendencies will be suddenly reversed.

If the view taken of Irish history in this brief sketch be correct, the original source of the calamities of Ireland was the partial character of the Norman Conquest, which caused the conquerors, instead of becoming an upper class, to remain a mere hostile settlement or Pale. This was an accident of history for which the descendants of the two races are as little responsible as they are for the accidents of geology. The next great source

of mischief was the disruption of Christendom at the
period of the Reformation, and the terrible religious
wars which ensued upon that disruption, and into which
both nations, in common with the other nations of
Europe, were drawn. Then Ireland became a victim
to the attempt of Louis XIV., which was in part a
sequel of the religious wars, to destroy the liberty and
religion of England through his vassals, the House of
Stuart. Finally, the French Revolution breaking out
into anarchy, massacre, and atheism, at the moment
when the Government of England under Pitt had just
entered on the path of reform and toleration, not only
arrested political progress in this as in other cases, but
involved Ireland in another civil war. Many of the
actors in these miserable events merited personal infamy which no reference to general causes can remove.
The governors of Ireland who treated the natives with
inhumanity, while they were humanely treated by contemporary governors, such as Sir John Perrot; the vile
adventurers, who plied the trade of confiscation under
the Stuarts; the members of Parliament and prelates
who were active in framing the Penal Code; the Irish
gentlemen and yeomanry who tortured and butchered
in 1798, cannot be saved by any philosophy of history
from everlasting shame. But if the question is between
the Irish and the English people, there is no part of
all this which may not be numbered with the general
calamities of Europe during the last two centuries, and
with the rest of those calamities buried in oblivion.
The theory of an exterminating policy, carried on by
one people against the other, is historically untenable.

It is also morally absurd. Individual men may be cold-blooded and systematic murderers; but a nation of cold-blooded and systematic murderers, is a thing which human nature has not yet produced. A man who should allow himself to entertain such a notion would have a very distempered imagination, and a man who should allow himself to be guided by it in action would certainly find that he had acted like a fool.

Still more does justice require that allowance should be made on historical grounds for the failings of the Irish people. If they are wanting in industry, in regard for the rights of property, in reverence for the law, history furnishes a full explanation of their defects, without supposing in them any inherent depravity or even any inherent weakness. They have never had the advantage of the training through which other nations have passed in their gradual rise from barbarism to civilization. The progress of the Irish people was arrested at an almost primitive stage, and a series of calamities following close upon each other has prevented it from ever fairly resuming its course. The pressure of overwhelming misery has now been relieved; government has become mild and just; the civilizing agency of education has been introduced; the upper classes are rapidly returning to their duty, and the natural effect is at once seen in the improved character of the people. Statesmen are bound to be well acquainted with the historical sources of the evil with which they have to deal, especially when those evils are of such a nature as, at the first aspect, to imply depravity in a nation. There are still speakers and writers who seem to think that the Irish are incurably vicious, because the accumulated effects of so many unhappy centuries cannot be removed at once by a wave of the legislator's wand. Some still believe, or affect to believe, that the very air of the island has in it something destructive of the characters and understandings of all who breathe it. These absurdities are of old standing. "Marry," says one of the speakers in Spenser's Dialogue, "so there have been divers good plots devised, and wise counsels cast already about reformation of that realm; but they say it is the fatal destiny of that land, that no purposes whatsoever which are meant for her good, will prosper or take good effect; which, whether it proceed from the very genius of the soil, or influence of the stars, or that Almighty God hath not yet appointed the time of her reformation, or that He reserveth her in this unquiet state still for some secret scourge, which shall by her come unto England, it is hard to be known, but yet much to be feared." "Surely," the other speaker is made to reply, "I suppose this but a vain conceit of simple men, which judge things by their effects, and not by their causes; for I would rather think the cause of this evil which hangeth upon that country, to proceed rather of the unsoundness of the counsels and plots which you say have been oftentimes laid for the reformation, or of faintness in following and effecting the same, than of any such fatal course appointed by God as you may misdeem; but it is the manner of men, that when they are fallen into any absurdity, or their actions succeed not as they would, they are always ready to impute the blame thereof unto the heavens; so to excuse their own follies and imperfections." Spenser had also often heard the wish expressed, even by wise men, "that all that land were a sea-pool," a kind of speech which he held "to be the manner rather of desperate men far driven, to wish the utter ruin of that which they cannot redress, than of grave councillors which ought to think nothing so hard, but that through wisdom it may be mastered and subdued, since the Poet saith that the wise man shall rule even over the stars, much more over the earth."

It may perhaps be added that the lateness of the Union between England and Ireland, though caused by, and connected with, all that is most deplorable, is not in itself altogether to be deplored. Early consolidation and perfect unity, are in one point of view sources of great strength to a nation, as we see in the case of France. But in another, and perhaps a more important point of view, a nation may derive advantage from the independent action of different elements in its composition down to a later period of its history. Wholesome checks are thus imposed upon tendencies which otherwise would become too exclusively dominant, and give a one-sided character to civilization; and questions are kept in some measure open, which would otherwise be prematurely closed. Nothing seems more lamentable to ordinary readers of history than the death of that heiress of Scotland who was destined to unite her country peacefully to England by marrying the heir of Edward I. No doubt a union, if it had taken place at that time, would have spared the two countries several centuries of bloody and desolating wars. Yet nothing contributed more than the distinct national character and the distinct religion of the Scotch, to save Britain from being entirely subjugated by the Absolutism of Strafford, and the Anglicanism of Laud. It was not in London, but in Edinburgh, that those conspirators first encountered a serious resistance. Ireland seems now to be performing for the empire a somewhat analogous service in a different way. By virtue of her long unsettlement and her special claims to consideration, she is affording a clear field for the discussion of political, ecclesiastical, and social questions which the English nation, satisfied with an early and limited progress, will not suffer to be mooted directly in respect to itself. An Irish famine repealed the Corn Laws. Irish outrage gave to the empire the benefit of a regularly organized police. The desperate state of Irish property led to the passing of an Encumbered Estates Act. Ireland has introduced the system of mixed education. In Ireland the relations between landlord and tenant have been first made the subject of discussion, with some prospect of an equitable solution. In Ireland was promulgated the potent aphorism, 'Property has its duties as well as its rights.' In Ireland, where the members of the dominant Church are in a small and hopeless minority, and the Establishment is clearly a political evil, the great question of Church and State will probably be first raised with effect, and receive its most rational solution.

By the same Author.

AN INAUGURAL LECTURE DELIVERED BEFORE THE UNIVERSITY OF OXFORD. 8vo., sewed, price 1s. 6d.

THE STUDY OF HISTORY. TWO LECTURES DELIVERED BEFORE THE UNIVERSITY OF OXFORD. 8vo., sewed, price 2s. 6d.

ON SOME SUPPOSED CONSEQUENCES OF THE DOCTRINE OF HISTORICAL PROGRESS. A LECTURE DELIVERED BEFORE THE UNIVERSITY OF OXFORD. 8vo., sewed, price 1s. 6d.

THE FOUNDATION OF THE AMERICAN COLONIES. A LECTURE DELIVERED BEFORE THE UNIVERSITY OF OXFORD. 8vo., price 1s.

The set in one Vol., cloth, 5s.

AN INAUGURAL LECTURE.
I. II. ON THE STUDY OF HISTORY.
III. ON SOME SUPPOSED CONSEQUENCES OF THE DOCTRINE OF HISTORICAL PROGRESS.
IV. ON THE FOUNDATION OF THE AMERICAN COLONIES.

OXFORD AND LONDON: J. H. AND JAS. PARKER.

WORKS ON
Mediæval Architecture and Archæology,

PUBLISHED BY

JOHN HENRY AND JAMES PARKER,
OXFORD; AND 377, STRAND, LONDON.

ARCHITECTURAL MANUAL.
AN INTRODUCTION TO THE STUDY OF GOTHIC ARCHITECTURE.
By JOHN HENRY PARKER, F.S.A. Second Edition, Revised and Enlarged, with 170 Illustrations, and a Glossarial Index. Fcap. 8vo., cloth lettered, price 5s.

"The attention which of late years has been given to Gothic Architecture, especially by men who are not professional architects, renders necessary some sure and safe guide to the study of the art. Such a book is that by Mr. Parker, a second edition of which has just made its appearance. The new matter and illustrations, incorporated with the old, combine to make it the most comprehensive and practically useful treatise upon the subject which can be placed in the hands of any one desirous of being taught the principles of Gothic structure. It was written, as the author says, not so much 'for architects as for their employers, the gentry and clergy of England.'"—*Art Journal.*

THE GLOSSARY OF ARCHITECTURE.

A Glossary of Terms used in GRECIAN, ROMAN, ITALIAN, and GOTHIC ARCHITECTURE. Exemplified by upwards of Eighteen Hundred Illustrations, drawn from the best examples. *Fifth edition*, 3 vols. 8vo., cloth, gilt tops, 1*l.* 10*s.*

A VOCABULARY OF GOTHIC ARCHITECTURAL TERMS, in FRENCH AND ENGLISH, and English and French, with references to the Engravings in the English Glossary. 8vo., 1*s.*

——— in GERMAN AND ENGLISH, and English and German. 8vo., 1*s.*

ARCHÆOLOGY.

MEDIÆVAL SKETCH-BOOK.
FACSIMILE OF THE SKETCH-BOOK OF WILARS DE HONECORT, AN ARCHITECT OF THE THIRTEENTH CENTURY. With Commentaries and Descriptions by MM. LASSUS and QUICHERAT. Translated and Edited, with many additional Articles and Notes, by the Rev. ROBERT WILLIS, M.A., F.R.S., Jacksonian Professor at Cambridge, &c. With 64 Facsimiles, 10 Illustrative Plates, and 43 Woodcuts. Royal 4to., cloth, 2*l*. 10*s*. *The English letterpress separate, for the purchasers of the French edition*, 4to., 15*s*.

MEDIÆVAL IRONWORK.
SERRURERIE DU MOYEN-AGE,
Par RAYMOND BORDEAUX.
Forty Lithographic Plates, by G. Bouet, and numerous Woodcuts. Small 4to., cloth, 20*s*.

MEDIÆVAL ARMOUR.
ANCIENT ARMOUR AND WEAPONS IN EUROPE. By JOHN HEWITT, Member of the Archæological Institute of Great Britain. Vols. II. and III., comprising the Period from the Fourteenth to the Seventeenth Century, completing the work, 1*l*. 12*s*.
Also Vol. I., from the Iron Period of the Northern Nations to the end of the Thirteenth Century, 18*s*.
The work complete, 3 vols., 8vo., 2*l*. 10*s*.

MEDIÆVAL BRASSES.
A MANUAL OF MONUMENTAL BRASSES. Comprising an Introduction to the Study of these Memorials, and a List of those remaining in the British Isles. With Two Hundred Illustrations. By the Rev. HERBERT HAINES, M.A., of Exeter College, Oxford; Second Master of the College School, and Chaplain of the County Asylum, Gloucester. (With the Sanction of the Oxford Architectural Society.) 2 vols., Medium 8vo., price 21*s*.

MEDIÆVAL MANNERS AND CUSTOMS.
OUR ENGLISH HOME: Its Early History and Progress. With Notes on the Introduction of Domestic Inventions. Second Edition. Crown 8vo., price 5*s*.

"It contains the annals of our English civilization, and all about our progress in social and domestic matters, how we came to be the family and people which we are. All this forms a book as interesting as a novel, and our domestic history is written not only with great research, but also with much spirit and liveliness."—*Christian Remembrancer.*

ARCHITECTURE.

WESTMINSTER ABBEY.

GLEANINGS FROM WESTMINSTER ABBEY. By GEORGE GILBERT SCOTT, R.A., F.S.A. With Appendices supplying Further Particulars, and completing the History of the Abbey Buildings, by W. Burges, M.R.I.B.A., J. Burtt, F.S.A., G. Corner, F.S.A., W. H. Hart, F.S.A., J. J. Howard, F.S.A., Rev. T. Hugo, M.A., F.S.A., J. Hunter, F.S.A., H. Mogford, F.S.A., J. H. Parker, F.S.A., Rev. M. Walcott, M.A., F.R.S., Rev. T. W. Weare, M.A., Rev. Professor Willis, M.A., F.R.S. Illustrated by numerous Plates and Woodcuts. 8vo., 7s. 6d.

NEW OXFORD MUSEUM.

THE OXFORD MUSEUM. Remarks addressed to a Meeting of Architectural Societies, by HENRY W. ACLAND, M.D., F.R.S., Regius Professor of Medicine; with Letters from JOHN RUSKIN, M.A., Honorary Student of Christ Church; and JOHN PHILLIPS, M.A., F.R.S., Reader in Geology. Second Edition. Fcap. 8vo., sewed, 1s.

MEDIÆVAL CASTLES.

THE MILITARY ARCHITECTURE OF THE MIDDLE AGES. Translated from the French of M. VIOLLET-LE-DUC, by M. MACDERMOTT, Esq., Architect. With 151 original French Engravings. Medium 8vo., cloth, 21s.

Also in the press, uniform with the above,

AN HISTORICAL AND ARCHITECTURAL ACCOUNT OF ENGLISH CASTLES. By the Rev. C. H. HARTSHORNE, M.A. With numerous Engravings.

MEDIÆVAL SCULPTURE.

A SERIES OF MANUALS OF GOTHIC ORNAMENT. Price 1s. each.

        No. 1. STONE CARVING.
        No. 2. MOULDINGS.
        No. 3. SURFACE ORNAMENT.

The Domestic Architecture

OF THE

Middle Ages.

Vol. I.—FROM WILLIAM I. TO EDWARD I. (or the Norman and Early English Styles). 8vo., 21s.

Vol. II.—FROM EDWARD I. TO RICHARD II. (the Edwardian Period, or the Decorated Style). 8vo., 21s.

Vol. III.—FROM RICHARD II. TO HENRY VIII., in Two Parts. 8vo., 1l. 10s.

With numerous Illustrations of Existing Remains from Original Drawings.

The Work complete, with 400 *Engravings and a General Index,* 4 *vols.* 8vo., 3l. 12s.

"Nothing could be more opportune than its completion while the question of 'Classic' and 'Gothic' is still pending with regard to the Foreign Office. What is the true national architecture of England, and of what is it capable? These volumes contain evidence which might open the eyes of Lord Palmerston himself. They might even do something to relieve that lower depth of denseness, which is represented by Mr. Tite and Mr. Coningham.

"The whole history, as traced out by Mr. Parker, shews the absurdity of the vulgar notion that Gothic is in some special way an ecclesiastical style. The truth is that the mediæval architects, like the architects of every other good period, Christian or heathen, built their religious buildings in exactly the same style as their secular ones. They built both in the only style they knew of, at least the only one they could work in—namely, the style of their own day. A church, a house, a castle, of the same date, are very different things in outline and proportion—that is the natural result of their several purposes; but in mere style, in mere architectural forms, they are exactly the same. No point can be more important to insist on just now than this, and Mr. Parker's book comes very opportunely to set it forth at length.

"It is a work of thorough research and first-rate authority on a deeply interesting and important subject."—*Saturday Review*, Nov. 26, 1859.

ARCHITECTURAL TOPOGRAPHY.

APPENDIX TO RICKMAN'S GOTHIC ARCHITECTURE,
OR, AN ARCHITECTURAL ACCOUNT
OF EVERY CHURCH IN

BEDFORDSHIRE, 2s. 6d.	CAMBRIDGESHIRE, 4s.
BERKSHIRE, 2s. 6d.	HUNTINGDONSHIRE, 2s. 6d.
BUCKINGHAMSHIRE, 2s. 6d.	OXFORDSHIRE, 2s. 6d.

SUFFOLK, *with Engravings*, 7s. 6d.

Its Dedication,—Supposed date of Erection or Alteration,—Objects of Interest in or near,—Notices of Fonts,—Glass, Furniture,—and other details.—Also Lists of Dated Examples, Works relating to the County, &c.

N.B. Each Church has been personally surveyed for the occasion by some competent antiquary.

THE MEDIEVAL ARCHITECTURE OF CHESTER.
By JOHN HENRY PARKER, F.S.A. With an Historical Introduction by the Rev. FRANCIS GROSVENOR. Illustrated by Engravings by J. H. Le Keux, O. Jewitt, &c. 8vo., cloth, 5s.

ARCHITECTURAL NOTICES of the CHURCHES in the ARCHDEACONRY of NORTHAMPTON. With numerous Illustrations on Wood and Steel. Royal 8vo., cloth, 1l. 1s.

DESCRIPTIVE NOTICES OF SOME OF THE ANCIENT PAROCHIAL & COLLEGIATE CHURCHES of SCOTLAND, with Woodcuts by O. Jewitt. 8vo., 5s.

THE ARCHITECTURAL HISTORY OF CANTERBURY CATHEDRAL. By Professor WILLIS, M.A., F.R.S., &c. 8vo., 52 Woodcuts, *many of them coloured*, 6s.

By the same Author.

THE ARCHITECTURAL HISTORY OF WINCHESTER CATHEDRAL. 8vo., with Woodcuts and Plan, 5s.

THE ARCHITECTURAL HISTORY OF YORK CATHEDRAL. With Woodcuts and Plan, 2s. 6d.

THE SCULPTURES OF WELLS CATHEDRAL. With an Appendix on the Sculptures of other Mediæval Churches in England. By C. R. COCKERELL, Esq., Professor, R.A. 4to., with numerous Illustrations, 21s.

WORKING DRAWINGS OF CHURCHES, WITH VIEWS, ELEVATIONS, SECTIONS, AND DETAILS.

WARMINGTON CHURCH. Royal folio, cloth, 10s. 6d.
    A fine thirteenth century Church. About 115 feet by 47.

SAINT LEONARD'S, KIRKSTEAD. Small folio, 5s.
    A small Church in the Early English style. 42 feet by 19.

MINSTER LOVELL CHURCH. Folio, 5s.
    A very elegant specimen of the Perpendicular style. To hold 350 persons.

LITTLEMORE CHURCH. *Second Edition*, with the designs of the painted Glass Windows. Folio, 5s.
    A small modern Church, in the Early English style. Size, 60 feet by 55, and 40 feet high. Cost 800*l*. Holds 210 persons.

SHOTTESBROKE CHURCH. Folio, 3s. 6d.
    A good and pure specimen of the Decorated style.

WILCOTE CHURCH. Folio, 3s. 6d.
    A small Church in the Decorated style. Size, 50 feet by 20. Estimated cost, 364*l*. Holds 160 persons.

ST. BARTHOLOMEW'S CHAPEL, OXFORD. Folio, 3s. 6d.
    A small Chapel in the Early Perpendicular style. Size, 24 feet by 16. Estimated cost, 228*l*. Holds 90 persons.

STRIXTON CHURCH. Folio, 5s.
    A small Church in the Early English style. Calculated for 200 persons; to cost about 800*l*.

OXFORD BURIAL-GROUND CHAPELS. Folio, 10s. 6d.
    1. Norman.   2. Early English.   3. Decorated.
    Separately, each 5s.

PUBLISHED BY THE OXFORD ARCHITECTURAL SOCIETY.
Sixpence per Sheet.

OPEN SEATS.
1. Headington.
2. Huseley.
3. Steeple Aston.
4. Stanton Harcourt, Ensham, &c.
5. Littlemore.

PATTERNS OF BENCH ENDS.
6. Steeple Aston. Sheet 1.
7. Ditto. Sheet 2.

OAK STALLS.
8. Beauchamp Chapel.
9. Talland, Beverley, &c.

FONTS.
10. Heckington, (*Decorated*).
11. Newenden, (*Norman*).

REREDOS.
12. St. Michael's, Oxford.

WINDOW TRACERY.
13. Rickman's Specimens. Sheet 1.
14. Ditto. Sheet 2.

PULPITS.
15. Wolvercot, (*Perpendicular*).
16. Beaulieu, (*Decorated*).
17. St. Giles', Oxford, (*Decorated*); with Coombe, (*Perpendicular*).

SCREENS.
18. Dorchester and Stanton Harcourt.

ARCHÆOLOGICAL WORKS.

THE TRACT "DE INVENTIONE SANCTÆ CRUCIS NOSTRÆ IN MONTE ACUTO ET DE DUCTIONE EJUSDEM APUD WALTHAM," now first printed from the Manuscript in the British Museum, with Introduction and Notes by WILLIAM STUBBS, M.A., Vicar of Navestock, late Fellow of Trinity College, Oxford. Royal 8vo., (only 100 copies printed), price 5s.; Demy 8vo., 3s. 6d.

ARCHÆOLOGICAL JOURNAL. With numerous Illustrations. 5 vols. 8vo., *with General Index.* Cloth, 2l. Nos. 1—20, each 2s. 6d.

PROCEEDINGS OF THE ARCHÆOLOGICAL INSTITUTE AT WINCHESTER, 1845. With numerous illustrations. 10s. 6d.

PROCEEDINGS AT NORWICH. 1847. 8vo. cloth, 10s. 6d.

A BOOK of ORNAMENTAL GLAZING QUARRIES, collected and arranged from Ancient Examples. By AUGUSTUS WOLLASTON FRANKS, B.A. With 112 Coloured Examples. 8vo., 16s.

SPECIMENS OF CHURCH PLATE, SEPULCHRAL CROSSES, &c. 4to., cloth lettered, 1l. 1s.

FAIRFORD GRAVES. A Record of Researches in an Anglo-Saxon Burial-place in Gloucestershire. By W. M. WYLIE, F.S.A. 4to., 10s. 6d.

A MANUAL for the STUDY of SEPULCHRAL SLABS and CROSSES of the MIDDLE AGES. By the Rev. EDWARD L. CUTTS, B.A. 8vo., illustrated by upwards of 300 Engravings. 6s.

AN ESSAY ON THE ORIGIN AND DEVELOPMENT OF WINDOW TRACERY IN ENGLAND. Illustrated by nearly 400 Examples. By EDWARD A. FREEMAN, M.A., late Fellow of Trinity College, Oxford. 8vo. cloth, 12s.

THE PRIMEVAL ANTIQUITIES OF ENGLAND AND DENMARK COMPARED. By J. J. A. WORSAAE. Translated and applied to the illustration of similar remains in England, by W. J. THOMS, F.S.A., &c. With numerous illustrations. 8vo. 5s.

The Gentleman's Magazine.

New Series—published monthly, price 2s. 6d.

WITH the year of our Lord 1859, *Sylvanus Urban* closed his 207th volume, and the 128th year of his literary existence. This is a length of days that, so far as he knows, has never before been attained by a Journalist; but he ventures to affirm, with thankfulness as well as some degree of self-complacency, that he is still in a green old age, and that to his thinking the time is yet very distant when, to borrow the words of one of his earliest and most valued friends, it may be said of him—"Superfluous lags the veteran on the stage."

The times, it is readily allowed, have greatly changed since *Sylvanus Urban* first solicited public attention, but it may be fairly doubted whether the tastes and habits of thought of the educated classes to whom he addresses himself have changed in a like degree. Hence he does not fear that History and Antiquities, in their widest sense, can ever become unpalatable to them, but, on the contrary, he is glad to mark an increased avidity in pursuing such studies. This is a state of things that he thinks he may claim a considerable share in bringing about, and the steady progress of which he is desirous of forwarding by all available means. He alludes to the growing appreciation of the Past, as the key to the understanding of the Present, and (in a sense) of the Future, as testified by the formation of Archæological and Literary Societies, which have already achieved much good, and may do still more; and as a means to that end, he devotes a portion of his pages every month, under the title of "ANTIQUARIAN AND LITERARY INTELLLIGENCER," to a record of their progress.

Sylvanus Urban therefore ventures to suggest to the Councils of such Societies, that if brief reports of their proceedings and publications are systematically supplied to the GENTLEMAN'S MAGAZINE, where they will be always highly acceptable, an interchange of knowledge and good offices may thus be established between learned bodies in the most distant parts of the Empire—an interchange that does not now exist, but the want of which few will be found to deny.

It has ever been the desire of *Sylvanus Urban* to see his CORRESPONDENCE a leading feature in his pages, and he has had the gratification of reckoning many of the most erudite men of the time as his fellow-workers, who have, through him, conveyed an invaluable amount of knowledge to the world. He invites those of the present day to imitate them. Another important feature has been, and will be, the OBITUARY, to the completeness of which he requests friends or relatives to contribute by communicating fitting notices of eminent persons daily removed by the hand of death from among us. He believes that he shall not be disappointed in the extent of this friendly co-operation, but that, on the contrary, the increasing number of his contributors will render the motto that he has so long borne more than ever applicable:—"*E pluribus Unum.*"

All Communications to be addressed to MR. URBAN,
377, STRAND, LONDON, W.C.

www.ingramcontent.com/pod-product-compliance
Lightning Source LLC
Chambersburg PA
CBHW020829230426
43666CB00007B/1156